North Carolina
as a
Civil War Battleground
1861 - 1865

JOHN GILCHRIST BARRETT

Raleigh
Division of Archives and History
North Carolina Department of Cultural Resources

NORTH CAROLINA DEPARTMENT OF CULTURAL RESOURCES
BETTY RAY MCCAIN
Secretary

ELIZABETH F. BUFORD
Deputy Secretary

DIVISION OF ARCHIVES AND HISTORY
JEFFREY J. CROW
Director

LARRY G. MISENHEIMER
Deputy Director

NORTH CAROLINA HISTORICAL COMMISSION
WILLIAM S. POWELL (2001)
Chairman

ALAN D. WATSON (2003)
Vice-Chairman

MILLIE M. BARBEE (2003)	MARY HAYES HOLMES (1999)	PERCY E. MURRAY (1999)
N. J. CRAWFORD (2001)	H. G. JONES (2001)	JANET N. NORTON (1999)
T. HARRY GATTON (2003)	B. PERRY MORRISON JR. (1999)	MAX R. WILLIAMS (2001)

© 1987 by the North Carolina Division of Archives and History
All rights reserved
Twelfth printing 1997
ISBN 0-86526-088-5

Zebulon Baird Vance (May 13, 1830-April 14, 1894) was elected governor in 1862 and in 1864. Before being elected governor he was colonel of the Twenty-sixth North Carolina Regiment and participated in the battles around New Bern and Kinston. After the war he again served as governor (1877-1879) and was later United States Senator (1879-1894).

Henry Toole Clark (1808-April 14, 1874) was president of the State Senate when the war began. Ellis died in July and Clark filled Ellis's unexpired term, but did not seek election to continue as governor.

John Willis Ellis (November 23, 1820-July 7, 1861) was governor when the Secession Ordinance of May 20, 1861, was passed. Ellis refused to send State troops on Lincoln's call but rather began to prepare to defend the State. He did not live to complete his term.

FOREWORD

In 1958 the agency then known as the State Department of Archives and History published a pamphlet titled *Pictures of the Civil War Period in North Carolina*. The pamphlet was later reissued under the title *Civil War Pictures* and has been reprinted numerous times. Demand for information on the Civil War increased, however, and the need for an authentic and well-written account of the war was felt. John G. Barrett, author of *Sherman's March through the Carolinas* and *The Civil War in North Carolina*, agreed to write a booklet on the subject; this publication is the result.

Dr. Barrett, a native of Scotland County, is a former professor of history at Virginia Military Institute. His doctorate in history is from the University of North Carolina at Chapel Hill.

The pictures reproduced in this volume are from various sources. Seventeen were used in *Pictures of the Civil War Period in North Carolina*. Some of those pictures were from *Harper's Weekly*; the *Pictorial War Record*; *Frank Leslie's Illustrated Newspaper*; the *Illustrated London News*; Benson J. Lossing's *A History of the Civil War*; *The American Soldier in the Civil War: A Pictorial History of the Campaigns and Conflicts of the War between the States, Profusely Illustrated . . . from Sketches by Forbes, Taylor . . . and Other Celebrated War Artists*; and Walter Clark, ed., *Histories of the Several Regiments and Battalions from North Carolina in the Great War, 1861-'65*. Mrs. Madlin M. Futrell, formerly a member of the staff of the North Carolina Museum of History, made the prints.

Mrs. Betsy J. Gunter, formerly on the staff of the Historical Publications Section, assisted in preparing the copy for the printer and in seeing the pamphlet through the press. She also produced the map folded in at the end of the pamphlet; the map shows most of the forts, towns, and battlefields mentioned in the study. Dr. Charles L. Price and John Conner Atkeson Jr. corrected and revised the map in 1980.

Joe A. Mobley, *Administrator*
Historical Publications Section

January 1998

CONTENTS

LIST OF ILLUSTRATIONS

Chapter I

NORTH CAROLINA LEAVES THE UNION

North Carolina, a State in the upper South, did not play a leading role in the great secession drama of 1860-1861. While the "fire-eaters" in South Carolina and the States of the lower South were talking secession, North Carolinians, for the most part, still favored the national Union. Since the soil of the State was not well suited for the growing of cotton, there were relatively few wealthy planters with large slaveholdings to agitate for a break with the federal government. The nonslaveholders from the mountain districts of the West, the swamp regions of the East, certain Quakers and small farm elements in the central region saw no reason to become vitally concerned with the preservation of a slave system in which they had little part.

The election of Abraham Lincoln to the Presidency of the United States in November, 1860, triggered the secession of the States of the lower South, but in North Carolina the majority of the people were still unionist. This majority did not regard Lincoln's election as sufficient grounds for a withdrawal from the Union. The general sentiment within the State was one of "watch and wait." Lincoln, it was thought, should be given a reasonable length of time to show his course of action.

North Carolina's governor, John W. Ellis, was not in the least surprised at his State's cautious approach to secession. Back in October, 1860, he had written Governor William Henry Gist of South Carolina that the people of North Carolina were far from being unanimous in their views and feelings concerning the action the State would take if Lincoln were elected President. Ellis said that some would yield, some would oppose his power, and others would probably adopt the "wait and see" attitude. Many of the people believed "he would be powerless for evil with a minority in the Senate and perhaps in the House of Representatives"; while others said, however, that his election "would prove a fatal blow to the institution of negro slavery in this country." The Governor did believe, however, that a majority of his people would not consider Lincoln's election "as sufficient ground for dissolving the Union of the States."

Even though Lincoln's election and the consequent secession of the "cotton states" did not bring about North Carolina's immediate withdrawal from the Union, it did create a crisis within the State. When the General Assembly met on November 19, it became apparent to all that the session was to be an exciting one. Almost immediately secession became a matter of grave debate. Governor Ellis's message to the Assembly was keenly awaited throughout the State. It was generally thought that the chief executive would outline the policy North Carolina was to follow in this time of crisis. His message, as was expected, was closely in accord with the thinking of the "secessionists or radicals, who favored immediate action by North Carolina. . . ." Those who opposed the Governor's program were generally classified as "unionists or conservatives." They saw no necessity for a withdrawal from the Union. Although Governor Ellis did not openly advocate secession, he did recommend that North Carolina call a conference with "those States identified with us in interest and in the wrongs we have suffered; and especially those lying immediately adjacent to us." After the meeting of this conference, he recommended that a convention of the people be called. He also made recommendations concerning a thorough reorganization of the militia.

In the General Assembly the radicals and conservatives hotly debated the great political issues of the day. Only on the matter of military preparedness did they seem to agree. Both factions felt that the State must prepare itself for any eventuality.

While the legislative halls resounded to heated debate, public opinion throughout the State was reaching fever pitch, due primarily to the growing strength of the secession movement. As early as November 12, 1860, a secession meeting was held in Cleveland County. A week later a similar gathering took place at Wilmington. Radical speakers throughout the State during November and December urged the call of a convention "of the people to determine upon a policy for the state."

In the midst of this agitation for a convention, South Carolina, on December 20, 1860, withdrew from the Union. In Wilmington, a secession stronghold, one hundred guns were fired in honor of the event. Only among the radicals, however, was South Carolina's action received with any true expression of joy. Conservative North Carolinians strongly condemned South Carolina for making this move and thereby rendering it more difficult for the other southern States to join in the movement.

Although South Carolina's action was strongly denounced in many quarters of North Carolina, the people of the State stood

James G. Martin graduated from the United States Military Academy at West Point in 1840. He served in the Mexican War and lost an arm at the battle of Churubusco. He resigned from the United States Army June 14, 1861, and joined the Confederate States Army. He served as adjutant general of North Carolina and deserves much credit for preparing the State for its defense and for supplies such as clothes, medicines, guns, ammunition, and other necessary war items. He was commissioned brigadier general May 15, 1862.

Weldon Nathaniel Edwards (1788-1873), native of Northampton County; educated at Warrenton Academy; practiced law in Warrenton; engaged in agricultural pursuits; protégé and kinsman of Nathaniel Macon; delegate to constitutional convention in 1835; staunch believer in right of secession; presided over first State meeting of secession party in 1861; chosen president of secession convention; wrote *Memoir of Nathaniel Macon of North Carolina* after his retirement.

united in opposing the use of force to bring the seceded State back into the Union. A contemporary expressed the feelings of many when he wrote: "I am a Union man but when they send men South it will change my notions. I can do nothing against my own people."

Two days after South Carolina's momentous decision the General Assembly of North Carolina adjourned for the Christmas season, the legislators not returning to Raleigh until January 7. During this period the conservatives of the State, noting the increasing disunion sentiment throughout the South, began to increase their activities. Many Union meetings were held, especially in the central and western parts of the State. The majority of those attending these meetings preferred to remain in the Union, if possible, but if attempts at compromise failed, they were willing to follow the lead of the other southern States.

Scarcely had the members of the General Assembly returned to their duties before the news came that the citizens of Wilmington and vicinity had seized Forts Caswell and Johnston near the mouth of the Cape Fear River. On December 31, 1860, the Wilmington citizens had wired Governor Ellis, requesting permission to seize these fortifications so vital to their city's welfare. The Governor refused the request on the grounds that he had no authority to grant such a request. The people, however, were not easily discouraged. On the first day of the new year, a commission from Wilmington headed by W. S. Ashe called on Ellis at Raleigh and begged for permission to take over the forts. The Governor again refused to go along with the request, and thus matters rested until January 8. On this date a dispatch was received in Wilmington stating that a United States "Revenue Cutter with fifty men and . . . eight guns . . ." was on its way to Fort Caswell. This news caused great excitement in the city and the next day the forts were seized. When Governor Ellis learned of this action, he demanded the immediate evacuation of the forts, as such a movement was without authority of law. The Governor then hastened to inform President James Buchanan of these events. This was done in order to give the President the true account and at the same time to secure information as to the Chief Executive's intentions with respect to garrisoning North Carolina forts. The President's reply came on January 15, through Joseph Holt, his Secretary of War. Holt assured Ellis that the President did not contemplate garrisoning the forts of the State.

The occupation and subsequent evacuation of Forts Johnston and Caswell aroused a great deal of excitement throughout North Carolina, as did the secession of four more States by January 19—Mississippi (on January 9, 1861), Florida (on January 10, 1861), Alabama (on January 11, 1861), and Georgia (on January 19, 1861). These developments put tremendous pressure on the General Assembly to call a convention. Conservative opposition dwindled, and on January 29 the Assembly adopted a bill directing the people to vote on February 28 on the question of calling a convention and to elect 120 delegates.

During the short preconvention campaign both the radicals and the conservatives worked hard to gain control of the convention. Much to the surprise of many people the vote on February 28 resulted in a victory for the conservatives. The proposal for a convention was defeated by a majority of 194.

Neither side, however, accepted the result as final. With the Washington Peace Conference a failure and secession an accomplished fact in the "Cotton States," both unionist and secessionist knew that North Carolina must soon make a definite decision on whether to join her sister States in secession[1] or to remain a part of the federal Union.

In April the course of outside events dictated the stand North Carolina would take. On April 13, 1861, Fort Sumter, after heavy bombardment, surrendered to the Confederate forces. North Carolina secessionists were thrilled by the accounts of this victory at Charleston. In Wilmington the news created the "wildest excitement." Radicals greeted the accounts with such expressions as "glorious news—glorious news." Unionists, on the other hand, were greatly saddened to learn that war had commenced. Bartholomew F. Moore of Raleigh commented at this time that "Civil War can be glorious news to none but demons or thoughtless fools, or maddened men."

On April 15 President Lincoln issued a call for 75,000 troops to suppress the southern "insurrection," and the Secretary of War wired Governor Ellis to furnish two regiments of militia for immediate service. To this wire the Governor replied immediately:

Your dispatch is received, and if genuine, which its extraordinary character leads me to doubt, I have to say in reply, that I regard the

---

[1] On February 4, 1861, delegates from the States of South Carolina, Georgia, Florida, Mississippi, Alabama, and Louisiana met at Montgomery, Alabama, to form the Confederate States of America.

levy of troops made by the administration for the purpose of sub-jugating the states of the South, as in violation of the Constitution, and as a gross usurpation of power. I can be no party to this wicked violation of the laws of the country and to this war upon the liberties of a free people. You can get no troops from North Carolina.

On the same day that Lincoln called for troops Governor Ellis ordered the occupation of Forts Caswell, Johnston, and Macon. The latter fort guarded Beaufort harbor. Orders were soon drawn up for the seizure of the United States Arsenal at Fayetteville and the United States Mint at Charlotte. A proclamation notifying the General Assembly to meet in special session on May 1 was also issued.

Public opinion now showed a sudden change—the entire State seemed to approve secession. Withdrawal from the Union was only a matter of time and the drafting of proper documents.

The extra session of the General Assembly met on May 1 and immediately passed a convention bill. The convention, which was to be unrestricted in powers and final in action, was to be composed of 120 delegates. The election was to be held on May 13, and the convention was to assemble on the 20th of May.

During the short period between the call for a convention and the election of delegates, there was no time for the alignment of factions. The only point of difference concerned the method by which the State should leave the Union and join the Confederacy.

The convention met as scheduled on May 20. Soon after the selection of Weldon N. Edwards as chairman of the body, an ordinance of secession was adopted. Within an hour the convention also passed an ordinance ratifying the Provisional Constitution of the Confederate States of America.

A member of the convention described the gathering as resembling "a sea partly in storm, partly calm, the Secessionists shouting and throwing up their hats and rejoicing, the Conservatives sitting quietly, calm, depressed." In the streets of Raleigh, people paraded and shouted for joy, bands played, church bells pealed, and guns fired salutes. For the secessionists it was a day of victory. For the old unionists, though, it was more a time of tragedy, certainly marking "the death knell of slavery."

Chapter II

PREPARATIONS FOR WAR

Although North Carolina was reluctant to leave the Union, once the move was made, there was no indecision in support of the Confederate States of America. The staunch unionist, John A. Gilmer of Guilford County, was correct when he remarked to a friend, after Lincoln's call for troops, "We are all one now." As a member of the new family of States, North Carolina threw her entire strength behind the southern cause.

In early May, 1861, the General Assembly, anticipating that the convention would pass an ordinance of secession, began preparations for war. Governor Ellis was given permission to offer to Virginia the service of North Carolina troops not immediately needed for coastal duty. A bill was passed authorizing the counties to make subscriptions for the purpose of arming and equipping volunteers. The statute requiring State officers to take an oath to support the Constitution of the United States was repealed. Authorization was given the Governor to raise ten regiments of State troops and fifty thousand volunteers. The State troops were to serve for the duration of the war and the volunteers for twelve months. A $5,000,000 bond issue was authorized to meet the initial expense of organizing and supplying the recruits.

In overwhelming numbers the youth of North Carolina responded to the Governor's call for troops. Training camps sprang up throughout the State. West Point graduates resigned their commissions in the United States Army to accept commissions in the State regiments. The task of organizing the twelve-months volunteers was at first entrusted to Colonel John F. Hoke and that of the State troops to Colonel James G. Martin. When Hoke resigned in the summer of 1861 to become colonel of the Thirteenth Regiment, Martin became Adjutant General for all the troops of the State. With speed and efficiency this one-armed veteran of the Mexican War began to prepare North Carolina troops for Confederate service.

The first State troops to leave for the Virginia front were commanded by Colonel D. H. Hill. By May 11 Colonel Hill had organized the First North Carolina Regiment, and within ten

Daniel Harvey Hill (July 12, 1821-September 24, 1889) was graduated from West Point in 1842. He participated in the Mexican War and was brevetted captain and later major. He resigned from the United States Army in 1849 to teach mathematics at Washington College, Virginia. In 1854 he became a professor at Davidson College and in 1859 was manager and commandant of the Military Institute at Charlotte. Hill was promoted to lieutenant general July 11, 1863, but his promotion was not sent to the Senate. He did serve with that title until the end of the war.

James Johnston Pettigrew (July 4, 1828-July 17, 1863) graduated from the University of North Carolina in 1847. He studied in Berlin and served as an assistant professor at the United States Naval Observatory, and was secretary of the Spanish Legation in 1850. He was colonel of the Twelfth Regiment North Carolina Volunteers and on February 26, 1862, was promoted to brigadier general. He was wounded at the Battle of Gettysburg, was wounded again at Falling Waters, and died at Bunker Hill.

days this command was on its way to Richmond. The departure of the First North Carolina from Raleigh was a colorful affair. Practically all the citizens of the capital city turned out to see the first North Carolina troops depart for the fort. With colors flying, ladies waving handkerchiefs, and the band playing "The Girl I Left Behind Me" and "Dixie," the men marched down Fayetteville Street on their way to the railroad cars that would take them to Virginia.

During these early months patriotism was at its height, as very few North Carolinians realized the tragedy of war. Young men left home for camps of instruction in the spirit of a holiday outing. The Warren County Guards and their ornately uniformed officers arrived at camp near Raleigh with a wagon train big enough to transport the baggage of an entire army corps. The type of the baggage was even more remarkable than the number of pieces. There were banjos, guitars, violins, huge camp chests, and even bedsteads. The young bloods of Warren County thus intended to enjoy the luxuries of home while in training.

Many of the early volunteers were unprepared, yet many of them developed into excellent soldiers. Much of the credit for this success must go to Adjutant General Martin. Under his "genius . . . recruiting, drilling, organizing, and purchasing all took 'form.' " The cost of raising an army, however, was staggering. On May 27 Governor Henry T. Clark, who had succeeded to office upon the death of Governor Ellis, informed the convention that the $5,000,000 appropriated by the General Assembly had already been spent and that an additional $6,500,000 was urgently needed. Though dismayed at the mounting cost of war, the lawmakers set about to find the needed funds. On June 27 part of the financial burden was shifted to other shoulders. On this date the State transferred her military and naval forces to the Confederacy.

The North Carolina navy was small indeed in 1861 but was destined to play a leading role in some of the early coastal fighting. The few ships in the fleet were jokingly called the "mosquito fleet."

The medical service of the State was organized before the passage of the ordinance of secession. On May 16 Dr. Charles E. Johnson had taken over as Surgeon General of North Carolina troops. He soon had hospitals at Raleigh, Weldon, Salisbury, Charlotte, Goldsboro, and Tarboro. In addition, he organized a nursing service. Before the war ended, Dr. Peter E. Hines and

Dr. Edward Warren also served as the chief medical officer of the State.

Although the women of North Carolina were never officially organized for war work, their contributions to the war effort were varied and tremendous. Not the least of the contributions came from the womenfolk of common soldiers. The majority of soldier wives in North Carolina "were rural nonslaveholding women," who could expect little or no money from their husbands' meager pay. It was up to these women, therefore, to find the means to support themselves and their dependents. The burdens these lowly people were called upon to bear were enormous. A North Carolinian described the women of his section as "heroically plowing, planting and hoeing while their babes ly on blankets or old coats in the corn rows."

During the early days of the war, equipment, not men, was desperately needed. The youth of State had flocked to the colors in response to the Governor's call for troops, but once in camp it was difficult to find arms for these volunteers. This shortage was somewhat lessened when the State took over the United States Arsenal at Fayetteville. Thirty-seven thousand pieces of armament were taken there. Many of these were muskets of the old flintlock type dating back to the American Revolution. As soon as workmen could be found who knew how to operate the machinery at the Arsenal, they were put to work changing the locks. In the meantime agents scoured the southern markets in search of firearms. In the State ordnance officers scraped together rifles of all sizes, shapes, and descriptions. In spite of these efforts arms were so scarce that some companies reported to the Virginia front without any arms while others were equipped with State manufactured pikes, which were wooden poles capped at one end with iron.

As for artillery, the picture was even darker. Besides several antiquated artillery pieces taken at the coastal forts and the Fayetteville Arsenal, North Carolina entered the war with only four old smoothbore cannons. These had been purchased from the military schools at Charlotte and Hillsboro. Recast church bells and scrap iron could not fill the need for making cannons; therefore, many artillery companies, like infantry units, left for the battle area without proper equipment.

It was necessary not only to arm but also to clothe the troops. In this field North Carolina was better prepared to fill her obligations. There were thirty-nine cotton and nine woolen mills in the State in 1861. The cloth from these mills was sent to the State clothing factory in Raleigh to be made into uniforms. The output of these mills was supplemented by the spinning efforts of the women back home. Eventually North Carolina undertook to clothe her own troops and, in so doing, not only bought the entire output of the mills in the State but also sent agents into the other southern States to buy cloth.

While agents from North Carolina traveled the South in search of arms and cloth, the State was "straining every energy to manufacture the necessary equipment and supplies." From the mountains to the sea, mills were established to produce the materials of war.

North Carolina's efforts to sustain an army in the field were tremendous, and in so doing, the resources of the State were strained to the limit. To supplement the State's provisions, supplies were brought in through the blockade. In April, 1861, President Lincoln had proclaimed a blockade of the South, but for quite some time it was not effective. During these early months many vessels slipped through the blockaders with ease to unload valuable cargoes at Wilmington. As the war continued, this port city became one of the main supply arteries for the Confederacy.

Chapter III

HATTERAS, AUGUST-DECEMBER, 1861

General Winfield Scott, Lincoln's aged military adviser, warned that the war would be long and costly, but the "hot-heads" of the North and South only "laughed at the absurdity of the old soldiers prediction." The opening military events seemed, however, to point to a quick southern victory. On June 10, 1861, at Big Bethel, near Yorktown, Virginia, a small Confederate force under Colonel John B. Magruder soundly defeated a much larger Federal army under General Benjamin F. Butler. Over half of Magruder's men belonged to D. H. Hill's First North Carolina Regiment. For raw recruits, Hill's men fought well on this hot summer day. They fought so well, in fact, that they received public thanks from both the Confederate Congress and the North Carolina Convention.

Bethel was little more than a skirmish, but in the South it aroused great enthusiasm. This victory was taken as proof that one Confederate soldier was equal to several northern troopers. In North Carolina the war spirit received a tremendous boost from this engagement. The convention with the sanction of the people moved ahead with a vigorous prosecution of the war.

North Carolinians now confidently expected another Confederate victory when General Irvin McDowell moved his Federal army out of the protective confines of Washington for a push on Richmond. These expectations of victory were justified on July 21 at Manassas Junction, Virginia. Here McDowell's army was routed and hurled back on the Nation's Capital by a Confederate force which included three North Carolina regiments.

The battle of First Manassas ended the major fighting in Virginia for the year 1861. North Carolina was not so fortunate, for during this lull after Manassas the Federal authorities turned their attention to the eastern part of the State.

The coast of North Carolina is indented by Currituck, Albemarle, Pamlico, Core, and Bogue sounds. Most of the rivers of the coastal plain—the Chowan, Roanoke, Tar-Pamlico, and Neuse-Trent—empty into these bodies of water. Federal military commanders realized early that the control of these sounds, with their navigable rivers, would mean the command of more

Major General Ambrose Everett Burnside (1824-1881), native of Indiana; graduated from West Point in 1847; served in Mexican and Indian wars; in January, 1862, sailed to Hatteras Inlet; captured Roanoke Island in February, 1862; occupied New Bern in March, 1862; Beaufort and Fort Macon besieged in April, 1862; commissioned major general, 1862; resigned commission in 1865 and held important positions in railroad and other corporations; governor of Rhode Island from 1866-1869; elected United States senator 1875-1881.

Major General Benjamin Franklin Butler (1818-1893), native of New Hampshire; graduated from Waterbury College in Maine; declared slaves contraband; was in command of military forces in a joint military and naval attack on the forts at Hatteras Inlet, took possession of, August 27 and 28, 1861; commanded land forces in capture of New Orleans, May, 1862; military governor of New Orleans, May to December, 1862, and by his arbitrary government, caused protest and charges of corruption; in command of districts of eastern Virginia and North Carolina in 1863; member of congress 1867-1875 and 1877-1879; prominent in impeachment of Andrew Johnson; governor of Massachusetts in 1883; the next year was unsuccessful candidate for President.

than one-third of the State and at the same time threaten the Wilmington and Weldon Railroad, the main line running south from Richmond.

To command the sounds, Federal forces first had to control the long sand bank which reached from near Cape Henry, Virginia, to Bogue Inlet below Beaufort, North Carolina. This long strip of sand, separating the sounds from the ocean and comprising two-thirds of the State's coast line, was at different intervals broken by narrow inlets. A few of these inlets provided safe passage from the usually turbulent Atlantic to the smooth inland waters.

Soon after seceding from the Union, North Carolinians made preparations to defend their coast. Two departments of coastal defense were created and put under the respective commands of Generals Walter Gwynn and Theophilus Holmes. These officers immediately began to strengthen existing fortifications and to build new ones. Fort Fisher[1] at the mouth of the Cape Fear River was begun as were forts at each of the unguarded inlets along the Outer Banks. Fort Oregon went up at Oregon Inlet, Fort Ocracoke (or Fort Morgan) just inside Ocracoke Inlet, and Forts Hatteras and Clark at Hatteras Inlet.

Hatteras and Clark were the most important of the above forts because they guarded the main inlet north of Beaufort. Fort Hatteras, the principal installation was located a short distance from the inlet and commanded the channel. Clark, a much smaller fort, was situated east of Hatteras and nearer the ocean.

As a second line of defense the State sent its "mosquito fleet" to the sounds. The captains of these small vessels were instructed to act not only in defense of the water but also to seize enemy shipping moving along the coast. The "Winslow" under Captain Thomas M. Crossan was singularly successful as a raider. Operating out of Hatteras for six weeks, she captured sixteen prizes.

In the early part of the summer before work on the forts was completed, General B. F. Butler suggested to the United States War Department that a small expedition be sent to Hatteras to destroy that "depot for . . . rebel privateers." The War Department seems to have paid little attention to Butler's suggestion, but the Navy Department was not long in seeing his wisdom. The outcome was a joint army-navy expedition against Hatteras,

---

[1] Fort Fisher was actually begun in April, 1861, with the construction of Battery Bolles which later became part of the larger works.

the navy under command of Commodore Silas H. Stringham and the army under General Butler. The primary objective of this expedition was to put a stop to the raiding activities of such vessels as the "Winslow" by first destroying Forts Hatteras and Clark and then by obstructing the channel. After this was done the entire force was to return to its base at Fortress Monroe, Virginia.

On August 26 a Federal squadron consisting of seven warships mounting 149 guns, steamed out of Hampton Roads. Accompanying the squadron was a fleet of transports carrying approximately 880 troops primarily of the Ninth and Twentieth New York Volunteers. By the afternoon of the 27th this naval force had arrived off Hatteras Inlet.

To oppose this array of men and ships, the Confederates had less than four hundred men under Colonel W. F. Martin. On the appearance of the Federal fleet, however, Martin sent word to Colonel G. W. Johnston at Portsmouth, sixteen miles distant, to hurry to Hatteras with reinforcements.

A Confederate lieutenant wrote his father at this time that "in all probability . . . tomorrow the rattle of musketry and the roar of cannon will be heard here. Old Abe has waited long, but at last has come, and one would suppose with the determination to break up this 'hornet's nest' at Hatteras."

The Lieutenant was correct. The Federal assault commenced on the morning of the 28th with a heavy bombardment of Fort Clark. Under cover of this fire 318 men of Colonel Max Weber's New York Regiment and two guns were landed up the beach. Only a heavy surf prevented more landings. The fleet kept up a heavy and accurate fire on the shore all day. Before noon, however, the defenders of Fort Clark, having exhausted their ammunition, were ordered to spike their guns, abandon the fort, and retire to Hatteras. After the Confederate withdrawal, Fort Clark was seized by Colonel Weber's men and the United States flag was raised over the fortification. To protect the men ashore, Admiral Stringham ordered the "Harriet Lane" and the "Pawnee" to lay near the beach.

As nightfall approached, rough weather forced the Admiral to withdraw his vessels for fear of wrecking them on the coast. This left Weber's small force at the complete mercy of the Confederate garrison at Hatteras. The soldiers and sailors of the Federal fleet were fully aware of this critical situation. Aboard the Admiral's flagship, a war correspondent wrote: "The feel-

The fleet opening fire in capturing the forts at Hatteras Inlet, August 28, 1861. Sketch by A. Waud. *Pictorial War Record*, January 21, 1882.

The interior of Fort Hatteras after the bombardment, August 29, 1861. Drawn by H. Sartorious. *Pictorial War Record*, February 4, 1882.

ing throughout the ship . . . was that we were beaten. . . . During the night the secessionists might make our soldiers prisoners, reinforce their own forts, repair damages, and be ready to show that they were not easily vanquished."

Ashore, the Federal officers and men discussed the possibility of capture and tried to make themselves comfortable in the rain. Colonel Weber, expecting an attack, posted pickets and deployed a detachment on the beach near Hatteras.

A short distance away Confederate spirits were high. About dusk Commodore Samuel Barron, Chief of Confederate Coastal Defenses, had landed with 230 reinforcements. After replacing Colonel Martin as commander of Hatteras, Barron detailed men to repair damages to the fort and made preparations for an attack on Fort Clark. Unfortunately for the State of North Carolina and the Confederate cause, a council of war did not appreciate the importance of such a raid. During the night, therefore, the Commodore gave up the idea and turned his attention to strengthening the defenses of Fort Hatteras.

When daylight came, the Federal fleet again moved into position and began to shell the fort. The weather was clear, the sea was calm, and the United States flag still flew over Fort Clark. Anchoring out of range of Hatteras' guns, the fleet began to pour "a storm of shells" on the fort. After three hours of this fire, Commodore Barron surrendered the fort and its entire garrison of over seven hundred men.

Throughout the North the news of this victory was received with great rejoicing. Coming so soon after the defeat at Manassas, it increased morale considerably.

The scene was different in the South. An angry Confederate Congress demanded the true story of Hatteras. In North Carolina, officials scrambled to lay the blame. In Raleigh a local paper asked the pertinent question: "Why did not our force of seven or eight hundred men kill, drive into the sea, or capture the enemy's force of 300 or 400 men who spent the night 600 yards of our troops?"

With Hatteras secure in his possession, General Butler took a second look at his orders, which were to abandon the place after blocking the inlet. Realizing the great importance of the Outer Banks, Butler decided to disobey his instructions and, upon departing for Fortress Monroe, to leave behind a force under Colonel Rush C. Hawkins to hold the inlet.

In the meantime Forts Ocracoke and Oregon had been abandoned by the Confederates without a fight. Within a few days, therefore, the Federal forces had gained control of the defenses guarding the inlets to Albemarle and Pamlico sounds. This was a serious blow to the Confederacy since it provided the enemy with a base for operations against eastern North Carolina.

A leading military figure of the North, writing afterwards, had this to say about the capture of Hatteras: "This was our first naval victory, indeed our first victory of any kind, and should not be forgotten. The Union cause was then in a depressed condition, owing to the reverses it had experienced. The moral effect of this affair was very great, as it gave us a foothold on Southern soil and possession of the Sounds of North Carolina. . . and ultimately proved one of the most important events of the war."

The fall of 1861 was a gloomy period for eastern North Carolinians. Outside of a minor victory at Chicamacomico, forty miles up the Outer Banks from Hatteras, and the capture of the Federal steamer "Fanny" in the same vicinity, there was little to cheer about. In addition, more than 250 residents of the Outer Banks took an oath of allegiance to the United States and promised to keep the Federals informed of Confederate movements. Those taking the oath declared that secret Union meetings were being held in the counties bordering Pamlico Sound and that many citizens were ready to avow openly the Union cause. Colonel Rush Hawkins, commanding at Hatteras, suggested to his superiors that a popular convention be held under the protection of the Federal army. Through such a convention, the Colonel thought, a third of the State could be restored to the Union at once.

The attitude of Hawkins and the Hatteras citizens raised Federal hopes that in eastern North Carolina might be found the nucleus for the organization of a "loyal government." In order to organize the unionists of the area, a "so-called" convention of the people was held at Hatteras in November, 1861. An ordinance proclaimed the Reverend Marble Nash Taylor provisional governor of North Carolina, and another declared the ordinance of secession null and void and instructed the governor to issue a call for a congressional election. The election was held and Charles H. Foster, a native of Maine and a Bowdoin College graduate, was elected to Congress. This whole Union movement

The bombardment of Fort Hatteras, Pamlico Sound, August 29, 1861, by the Federal fleet under Commodore Silas H. Stringham. Sketch by Theodore Kaufman. Frank Leslie's Illustrations in *The American Soldier in the Civil War.*

The United States frigate "Sabine," off Cape Hatteras, rescuing Major Reynolds' battalion of marines from the sinking steamer "Governor," November 2, 1861. Frank Leslie's Illustrations in *The American Soldier in the Civil War.*

was so deceptive, however, that Foster was never seated and Taylor's duties as provisional governor were short-lived.

The Federal authorities, while attempting to restore North Carolina to the Union, were at the same time attempting to raise troops in the eastern counties. In this effort they were not highly successful. The chief aid they received was from certain parties whom the Confederates called "Buffaloes." Although the "Buffaloes" considered themselves Union men, very few ever did any fighting. Their activities were confined primarily to robbery and pillage. When the Federal authorities called them "to the field," most of them "took to the woods" instead.

The failure of the Hatteras government and the attitude of the "Buffaloes" convinced the Federal government by the end of 1861 that its objectives in North Carolina, for the time being at least, should be military rather than political.

Chapter IV

THE BURNSIDE EXPEDITION, JANUARY-JULY, 1862

During the fall of 1861 Governor Clark was bombarded with petitions from the citizens of eastern North Carolina asking protection for their part of the State. With the capture of Hatteras it became obvious to most of these people that a major battle would soon be fought for the control of coastal Carolina. There was little question but that the scene of this engagement would be Roanoke Island. This historic little strip of land, commanding the entrance to Albemarle Sound, was the key to eastern North Carolina.

Governor Clark, nevertheless, could promise the people little. The State's coastal defenses were now under Confederate control, and all the Governor could do was to press upon the authorities at Richmond the need for troops. He pressed his case in vain. The War Department replied that all trained men were needed in Virginia. For North Carolina duty only newly recruited troops were available. To whip these recruits into a fighting force, Richard C. Gatlin, who had recently resigned his commission in the United States Army, was made a brigadier general and given command of the Department of North Carolina. General D. H. Hill was placed in charge of the defenses of Albemarle and Pamlico sounds. At Wilmington General Joseph R. Anderson took over command.

The Federal authorities planned to take Roanoke Island and from there push into the interior of the State by way of Goldsboro and Raleigh. By following this route Confederate communications south of Richmond could be cut. Also, Federal troops would be in position for a flank movement when General George McClellan drove the Confederates out of their capital city.

Hill and Gatlin were aware of these plans and did what they could to meet the emergency, but the means at hand were woefully inadequate for the task. General Hill, feeling that he could accomplish little, resigned his post and reported to Virginia. His former command was then divided between Generals Henry A. Wise of Virginia and L. O'B. Branch of North Carolina. Wise was put in charge of the region between Norfolk and Roanoke Island, and Branch the district extending from the island to New Bern. General Wise had less than fifteen hundred men un-

Right:

Colonel John Franklin Hoke (1820-1888), native of Lincolnton; graduated from the University of North Carolina in 1841; practiced law; uncle of Major General Robert F. Hoke; captain in Mexican War; served in several legislatures; appointed adjutant general of North Carolina in 1861 serving until the ten regiments of "State Troops" and thirteen regiments of "Volunteers" were organized and equipped; July, 1861, elected colonel of the Thirteenth (later Twenty-third) North Carolina Volunteers; in 1864, elected colonel of the Seventy-third Regiment, Senior Reserves. The close of the war found him guarding prisoners at Salisbury.

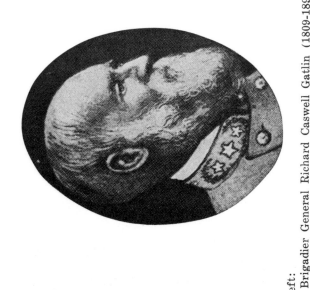

Left:

Brigadier General Richard Caswell Gatlin (1809-1896), native of Lenior County; attended University of North Carolina 1824-1825; graduated from West Point in 1832; fought in Seminole and Mexican wars; joined Confederate army and commanded coastal defense of the Southern Department; named brigadier general in July, 1861. While preparing for defense of New Bern, he became seriously ill. Resigned from active duty in September, 1862, and served as adjutant and inspector general.

der his command, and the majority of these were raw recruits, poorly equipped. At New Bern, ninety miles away, Branch had seven regiments.

The Federal expedition dispatched to capture Roanoke Island sailed from Hampton Roads on January 11, 1862. The fleet was under the command of Admiral L. M. Goldsborough and the landing force of fifteen thousand men was under General Ambrose P. Burnside. After a stormy voyage the vessels arrived off Hatteras Inlet. Heavy seas kept the fleet outside for several more days, and when passage through the inlet was attempted, many ships ran aground. Once inside Pamlico Sound it was necessary for the fleet to anchor for repairs; therefore, it was not until the morning of February 7 that the Federal squadron neared Roanoke Island.

This delay helped the Confederates very little. When the Federal ships finally appeared on the horizon, the island's defenses were still woefully weak. On the west side of the island were three forts—Huger, Blanchard, and Bartow—but only the most southern (Bartow) became actively engaged in the battle; the others were out of range. Across the sound on the mainland, the Confederates sank an old canal boat in the mud and mounted eight guns on her deck. This battery was called Fort Forrest. To protect the east side of the island, a two-gun emplacement was erected at Ballast Point. In the center of the island was a small three-gun battery (Fort Russell) commanding the only road running the length of the island. The battery was protected on each flank by marshes and deep cypress swamps.

Scattered about Roanoke Island in these different fortifications, the small Confederate force awaited the arrival of the Federal fleet. In command of the 1,434 Confederate effectives was Colonel H. M. Shaw; General Wise at the time was confined to his bed at Nags Head. The "mosquito fleet" under Commodore W. F. Lynch took position above Fort Bartow and behind some piles that partly obstructed the narrow channel through Croatan Sound.

By 11:00 A.M. on the 7th, the Federal gunboats were commencing to bombard the forts and to engage the Confederate fleet. While this duel between the heavy guns was in progress, General Burnside landed his infantry at Ashby Harbor about three miles below Fort Bartow. By nightfall the troops had made this lodgement secure. Early the next morning they began a concentrated attack on the battery situated in the center of the island.

The battery's defenders, however, opened up such a hot fire that the Federals could not advance up the narrow causeway. In the meantime Burnside's supporting forces arrived and began a flanking movement. The Confederates, thinking their flanks impenetrable, were completely surprised by the sudden appearance of men in blue on both sides. Unable to cope with this superior force, the small Confederate band retreated to the northern end of the island and there, along with the remainder of Colonel Shaw's troops, surrendered to the enemy.

On the previous night Commodore Lynch's "mosquito fleet" had steamed away from Roanoke Island. Having expended all of his ammunition and under orders "to defend the home waters," the Commodore had decided to take a position at Elizabeth City across Albemarle Sound. On the 10th, units of Admiral Goldsborough's fleet, sent in pursuit of Lynch, arrived at Elizabeth City. The Union vessels easily pushed aside the Confederate "fleet" and captured the town.

On the 11th Edenton was visited by a small Federal naval squadron, but the town suffered only the loss of some wheat and cotton. Winton, up the Chowan River, was not so fortunate. On the 20th Colonel Hawkins's Ninth New York burned much of the village.

After the fall of Roanoke Island, Burnside was in a position to move on New Bern, the second largest city on the North Carolina coast. For the defense of this strategic city, General Branch had approximately four thousand untried troops. His line of defense south of New Bern was anchored on the east by Fort Thompson and on the west by a swamp. This line was approximately two and one-half miles long and extended from the right bank of Neuse River to the Weathersly road. From the fort to the Atlantic and North Carolina Railroad, a distance of one mile, Branch posted four North Carolina regiments and a battalion of militia. Across the railroad Colonel Zebulon B. Vance's Twenty-sixth North Carolina was in position. Between Vance's left and a brick kiln along the railroad there was a break in the line. The night before the battle General Branch ordered two "twenty-four pounders" for this spot. The guns were not in place, however, when the fighting started, and consequently the battle was ultimately lost to Branch.

On March 13 approximately eight thousand troops of Burnside's command disembarked at Slocum's Creek below New Bern to begin a march on the city. Because of the rainy weather and

The interior of Fort Bartow during the bombardment, February 7, 1862. *Frank Leslie's Illustrated Newspaper*, March 8, 1862.

An explosion of a cannon on board the gunboat "Hetzel" at Fort Bartow, Roanoke Island, February 7, 1862. Sketch by J. Bentley. *Pictorial War Record*, July 15, 1882.

Charge of Hawkins's Zouaves on the Confederate batteries at Roanoke Island (Captured February 8, 1862). *Harper's Weekly,* March 1, 1862.

The 9th New York (Hawkins's Zouaves) and the 21st Massachusetts regiments taking, at the point of the bayonet, the Confederate fieldwork on Roanoke Island, February 8, 1862. *The Illustrated London News,* March 22, 1862.

the poor condition of the roads, the troops did not make contact with the Confederates on this date. Early the next morning, though, Burnside had his army in motion for New Bern. For the advance he divided his force into three columns. General John G. Foster commanded on the right between the river and the railroad, General Jesse L. Reno on the left of the railroad, and General John G. Parke in the center along the railroad, ready to aid either column. In support of Burnside was a fleet of gunboats on the Neuse. These vessels vigorously shelled the Confederate earthworks as the army advanced. Foster made contact on the Confederate left, only to have his frontal assault easily repulsed. Moving on the Confederate right, Reno found the break in Branch's line at the brickyard, charged through, turned to the right, and began to pour a deadly fire into the flank of the militia. These green troops retreated in confusion, soon to be followed by Colonel James Sinclair's Thirty-fifth North Carolina Regiment. General Branch rushed in troops to stem the breakthrough, which they did gallantly for a time. The Federals, however, continued to pour through the gap at the brick kiln and the defenders were unable to hold their ground. General Branch, outnumbered two to one and now with a break in his defenses, ordered his forces to retire toward Kinston. Before the day was over, New Bern was in Federal hands, and thus it remained for the duration of the war.

General Burnside had scarcely established his position in New Bern before word reached him that the Confederates were building ironclads at Norfolk and intended bringing them to the Albemarle region through the Dismal Swamp and Currituck canals. To block this supposed move, Burnside ordered General Reno to move up to South Mills on the Dismal Swamp Canal, blow up the lock located there, and then "proceed up to the head of Currituck canal and blow in its banks." General Reno moved his command, three thousand strong, from New Bern to Elizabeth City by water. From this latter place he marched north to South Mills, where, on April 19, he encountered the enemy under Colonel A. R. Wright. The Confederate commander had selected his defensive position with such care that for over three hours his seven-hundred-man force withstood all Federal assaults. Late in the day, though, Wright withdrew his men to a new position a mile in the rear. The Federals did not pursue and after nightfall made a hurried march back to their boats, leaving behind their dead and wounded.

By the time General Reno got back to New Bern with his men, another Federal force under General Parke was preparing a move on Fort Macon situated on Bogue Banks. This old style casemated work guarded Beaufort Inlet, the only entrance through the Outer Banks still not in Federal hands. In order to carry out his master plan of moving against Goldsboro and Raleigh and eventually Wilmington, General Burnside had first to reduce this one remaining Confederate stronghold to his rear. To assist in the reduction of the fort, the United States Navy already had cruisers patrolling off Beaufort.

Between March 18 and March 23, as a preliminary to the attack on Fort Macon, a Federal force had moved by land from New Bern to Beaufort, occupying along the way Havelock Station, Carolina City, Morehead City, and finally Beaufort. When this latter place fell to the Federals, serious preparations for the assault were started by General Parke. Heavy guns were floated to Bogue Banks on two-masted scows. Under cover of darkness these cannon and mortars were formed into batteries and placed twelve to fourteen hundred yards from Fort Macon. Rifle pits were dug about two thousand feet from the Confederate stronghold after attempts to place them closer were halted by accurate fire from the fort.

When General Parke felt strong enough to capture the fort, he offered Colonel Moses J. White, in command of the Confederate garrison, an opportunity to surrender. The Colonel politely refused despite the fact that he had fewer than three hundred men fit for duty.

In the clear dawn of April 25 the Federal troops fired the first round of an eleven-hour bombardment. The Confederates, without mortars to lob shells, were able to damage the Federal emplacements very little. Horizontally fired cannon of the fort were not very effective. Union steamers, unaware that the attack was to start that day, did not enter the battle until 8:20 A.M., and then the fort's accurate fire and heavy sea forced their retirement an hour later.

The most notable fact of the bombardment was the accuracy of the Union batteries. Out of 1,100 shots fired, 560 hit the fort. The credit for this remarkable feat must go to the Federal signal officer in Beaufort. Possessing an understanding of artillery fire, this officer was able to observe where the shells hit, and then to forward his corrections by flags to the batteries on the bank.

Bivouac in Fort Bartow the night after the capture of Roanoke Island, February 9, 1862. Sketch by J. Bentley. *Pictorial War Record*, July 22, 1882.

Confederate prisoners taken on Roanoke Island in 1862. Sketch by J. Bentley. *Pictorial War Record*, July 22, 1882.

Ruins of Winton, February 20, 1862. Sketch by F. C. H. Bonwill. *Frank Leslie's Illustrated Newspaper*, October 24, 1863.

The charge of the Hawkins Zouaves on a battery at South Mills near Elizabeth City, April 19, 1862. *Pictorial War Record*, September 9, 1882.

The United States Navy co-operating with the land forces in the attack on Fort Macon, April 20, 1862. Sketch by F. H. Schell. *Pictorial War Record*, September 16, 1882.

The capture of Fort Macon, April 26, 1862. Notice that the Confederate flag is being lowered on the flagpole. From a sketch by F. H. Schell, artist for *Leslie's Illustrated Weekly*.

Around four o'clock the firing ceased and a truce went into effect. Colonel White realized that further resistance would be futile. The next morning he went aboard General Burnside's schooner "Alice Price" where he signed the articles of capitulation. Before noon on this date the Fifth Rhode Island marched into Fort Macon, hauled down the Confederate flag, and raised the Stars and Stripes. So again this bastion became the property of the United States government. Until the close of the war, Beaufort harbor served as a coaling station for Federal blockaders.

With the capture of Roanoke Island, New Bern, and Fort Macon, Federal gunboats were able to control most of the waterways of eastern North Carolina. This made it a fairly simple matter for troops to occupy the surrounding area. Washington, Plymouth, and other eastern towns fell to the invaders in the spring of 1862.

The Federal occupation of the coastal regions was made easier in some instances by the strong Union sentiment that prevailed in many sections of the eastern counties. This unionism induced President Lincoln, for the second time, to attempt the establishment of a "loyal government" in eastern North Carolina. In May, 1862, he appointed Edward Stanly military governor of the State. The new governor was a native North Carolinian but at the time was living in California. Stanly established himself at New Bern and at once began the hopeless task of "leading the people back to the Union." He soon found himself in the unpleasant position of being a sincere unionist but at the same time abhorring the conduct of the Federal troops around him. Finally, in January, 1863, he resigned his position with a bitter attack on Lincoln's Emancipation Proclamation.

General Burnside's victories in eastern North Carolina were a severe blow to the South. The Confederate army in Virginia was now threatened by a striking force in its rear. The back door by inland waters to Norfolk was tightly shut causing the eventual evacuation of the city. Moreover, eastern North Carolina was a rich farming region, and its seizure meant a consequent loss of foodstuffs for the Confederacy.

Chapter V

EASTERN NORTH CAROLINA RAIDS, JULY-DECEMBER, 1862

General Burnside, after making things secure at New Bern, began preparations for a move on Goldsboro. Before the General could launch this campaign, he was ordered "to hurry with all speed" to the aid of General George McClellan, who was having difficulty at Richmond. General John G. Foster was left behind to hold the Federal gains in North Carolina. Foster's task was made easy by the fact that the Confederates, too, were withdrawing troops from the State for service in Virginia.[1]

Upon assuming command of the Federal forces in eastern North Carolina, General Foster immediately began the construction of fortifications at New Bern and the other places held by his troops. When these fortifications were completed, the General did not intend to remain inactive behind them but to reconnoiter the surrounding country. In this way he hoped to gain topographical information and at the same time to keep the enemy stirred up. In carrying out this plan, the Twenty-seventh and the Seventeenth Massachusetts proceeded by different roads to Pollocksville on the Trent River making a circuit of fifty miles and engaging the Confederates at several points. General Foster also had the area south of New Bern and the region between Plymouth and Washington thoroughly scouted. To inconvenience the enemy, Foster had the Confederate saltworks at Currituck and Bogue inlets destroyed. On October 31 the General himself led a five-thousand-man force out of New Bern for a raid on Tarboro. By November 12 he was back at his base, having gotten no closer than ten miles to his objective.

In the meantime a small Confederate force under Colonel S. D. Pool surprised the Federal garrison at Washington. After a "hot fight" in the streets of the town, Pool's men withdrew but took with them several pieces of artillery. In early December

---

[1] After the fall of New Bern there had been a change of command in North Carolina. General Gatlin was replaced by T. H. Holmes. General Robert Ransom was detached from the army in Virginia and ordered to report to Holmes. Aided by Generals Ransom, S. C. French, and J. R. Anderson, Holmes had reorganized his forces and built up their number by the end of March to 25,000. By July, however, there remained only four infantry regiments in the State.

The battle at New Bern and the repulse of the Confederates, March 14, 1863. Sketch by Edwin Forbes. *Harper's Weekly*, April 11, 1863.

Colored troops, under General Edward A. Wild, liberating slaves. *Harper's Weekly*, January 23, 1864.

The interior of the principal Confederate fortifications near New Bern, after their capture by forces under General A. E. Burnside, March 14, 1862. Sketch by F. H. Schell. *Frank Leslie's Illustrated Newspaper*, April 19, 1862.

The headquarters of Vincent Collyer, superintendent of the poor at New Bern, distributing captured Confederate clothing to the contrabands. Sketch by F. H. Schell. *Frank Leslie's Illustrated Newspaper*, June 14, 1862.

Military governor, Edward Stanly, entering Washington. Sketch by Angelo Wiser as it appeared in *Harper's Weekly*, July 19, 1862.

Edward Stanly was born in New Bern, but lived in Beaufort County after being licensed to practice law. He represented his district in Congress from 1839 to 1843. He was living in California when President Lincoln appointed him military governor, March 19, 1862, after Federal troops had captured the territory in and around Beaufort, New Bern, and Washington.

Negro volunteers passing the Broad Street Episcopal Church, New Bern. Sketch by F. H. Schell. *Frank Leslie's Illustrated Newspaper*, February 27, 1864.

Plymouth was also temporarily taken by the Confederates. On the morning of the 10th a combination force of infantry, artillery, and cavalry surprised the Federal pickets at Plymouth and then rushed into the town. The raiders "with a full allowance of the 'rebel yell' " scattered the enemy line drawn up across Main Street. After several hours, when the town was in partial ruins, the Confederates withdrew.

Raids such as these on Washington and Plymouth did not put General Foster on the defensive for long. During the fall months reinforcements poured into New Bern, and by December Foster was strong enough to make a major move on Goldsboro in an effort to cut the line of the Wilmington and Weldon Railroad where it crossed Neuse River. This expedition was to be in conjunction with the Federal advance on Fredericksburg.

Two days before Burnside, now commanding the Army of the Potomac, sent his troops against the Confederacy's impregnable defenses at Fredericksburg, Foster marched out of New Bern with a force of approximately eleven thousand men; his destination was the railroad bridge over Neuse River at Goldsboro. The Federal army met with little opposition until it reached Southwest Creek near Kinston. Here General Foster found the bridge across the creek destroyed and a Confederate force with artillery on the opposite bank. Since the creek was not fordable at this point, the Ninth New Jersey and Eighty-fifth Pennsylvania were ordered to cross as best they could. By felling trees, by swimming, by fragments of the bridge, and by an old mill dam these two regiments crossed the steam and dislodged the Confederates.

General G. N. Evans, commanding the Confederate forces, next took up position on Neuse River about two miles from the Kinston bridge. He posted his men in a strong wooded position, "taking advantage of the ground, which formed a natural breastwork." His right flank was protected by a deep swamp and his left by a bend in the river. In this strong position, Evans still was not able to withstand Foster's superior numbers. After a two and one-half hour battle on the 14th, the Confederates were forced back across the river. So near were the Federals that about four hundred of Evans's command were captured before they could cross the bridge. This structure had been fired by the retreating Confederates, but the flames were easily extinguished by the onrushing Federals. In spite of this reverse, General Evans reformed his broken ranks and prepared a new line of battle about two miles beyond Kinston. General Foster sent the Confederate officer a demand for surrender. As it was declined, the Federals made ready for an attack. But, before this offensive could get underway, the Confederates retired. Foster decided not to pursue and that night bivouacked his troops in a field near the town. While here he not only learned that Burnside had been defeated at Fredericksburg but also that Confederate reinforcements were being rushed to North Carolina. In spite of these disturbing bits of news, Foster decided to move on to Goldsboro and to do as much damage to the railroad as possible before returning to New Bern. The next morning, the 15th, the Federals crossed the Neuse and took the river road for Goldsboro.

On the 16th Foster arrived at Whitehall, eighteen miles from Goldsboro. There he found the bridge burned and General B. H. Robertson, of Evans's command, posted on the opposite bank of the river ready for battle. After making a strong feint as if to rebuild the bridge and to cross the Neuse, Foster moved on towards Goldsboro with the main body of his force. A few sharpshooters were left behind to keep the Confederates occupied.

By Wednesday morning of the 17th the Federals had reached the railroad a few miles from Goldsboro. From this point Foster sent a detachment of cavalry to nearby Dudley Station and Everettsville to destroy railroad property. At the same time, Foster's main force moved against the railroad bridge over the Neuse just south of Goldsboro. This important crossing was guarded by troops under General Thomas L. Clingman and was covered from a nearby hill by several pieces of artillery. After two hours of heavy fighting, the Federal column got close enough to the bridge to enable a soldier to dash forward and fire the structure. After the destruction of the bridge, General Foster gave orders for a return to New Bern.

Even though the Federals had managed to destroy the railroad bridge and rip up much track, the raid could be termed only a partial success. The injury to the Wilmington and Weldon line turned out to be only superficial. Within a few days Confederate engineers had repaired much of the damage. A new bridge was constructed over the river, and the road was in operation again in less than two weeks.

Chapter VI

D. H. HILL DEMONSTRATES AGAINST NEW BERN AND WASHINGTON, MARCH-APRIL, 1863

After his great victory at Fredericksburg, General Lee detached General James Longstreet, with two divisions, and sent him south. Longstreet's orders were to protect the supply lines in eastern North Carolina and at the same time to gather provisions from this fertile region. In order that the Confederate supply trains could move unmolested through the rich corn country east of the Chowan River, it was necessary to keep the enemy confined to his bases in tidewater Virginia and eastern North Carolina. In pursuance of this plan, therefore, Longstreet organized in Virginia a move on Suffolk, while D. H. Hill, his subordinate in North Carolina, planned demonstrations on New Bern and Washington.

General Hill's strategy for the New Bern operation called for a three-pronged attack on the city. General Junius Daniel's brigade at Goldsboro was to move on New Bern by the lower Trent road, the cavalry at Kinston under General B. H. Robertson by the upper Trent road, and General James Johnston Pettigrew at Magnolia with fifteen pieces of artillery by the Barryton Ferry road. Robertson's orders were to break up the Atlantic and North Carolina Railroad. Pettigrew's instructions were to shell Fort Anderson on the Neuse and any gunboats in the river.

On March 13 Daniel encountered and took the enemy's first line of works at Deep Gully about eight miles from New Bern.[1] At daylight on Saturday the Federals made a feeble attempt to recapture their entrenchments of the previous day but were easily repulsed. The two Confederate successes at Deep Gully, however, could not be followed up, as General Pettigrew found it impossible to carry Fort Anderson. Pettigrew began his bombardment on the 14th but soon realized that his artillery and ammunition "were worthless and unsuited to the work at hand. . . ." General Robertson, on the other hand, had not done much toward destroying the railroad. Hill had this to say about his cavalry chief: "Robertson sent me out a lieutenant, who

---

[1] General Hill, riding with Daniels's brigade at the time, then sent word to Robertson to make his move against the railroad the next day.

partly cut the railroad. He sent out a Colonel who saw some Yankees and came back. Robertson did not go himself. We must have a better man."

The failure of Robertson and Pettigrew to carry their objectives caused Hill to withdraw his forces from New Bern. Under orders, though, to demonstrate against Washington as well as New Bern, General Hill immediately began preparations for a move on the former place. By March 30 he had the town under siege. Along the Tar-Pamlico River, batteries were erected to engage the Federal gunboats and to check any attempt to reinforce the city by water. South of the river, Hill stationed mainly the troops of General Pettigrew, while north of this body of water R. B. Garnett's Virginians invested the town.

When General Foster learned that the Confederates planned an attack upon Washington, he immediately left New Bern with several members of his staff for the Tar-Pamlico River town, arriving there just ahead of the enemy forces. With great energy he began to strengthen existing fortifications and to build new ones. At the same time he sent direct appeals to New Bern for relief. In answer to Foster's cry for help, General Henry Prince moved a force by steamer to the mouth of the Pamlico where one look at the battery at Hill's Point made him so "sick at his stomach" that he returned to New Bern. A short time later General Spinola, moving overland to the relief of Washington, was also turned back, this time by Pettigrew at Blount's Creek. It was left to the Fifth Rhode Island to crack initially the Confederate defenses. On April 13 a gunboat carrying the New Englanders slipped past Fort Hill and made its way safely to the beleaguered city. The next day a transport ran the blockade.

The arrival of fresh supplies and troops made the capture of Washington by siege, as ordered by Lee and Longstreet, extremely unlikely. His objective now out of reach, Hill began to remove his forces on April 15. This marked the end of the siege of Washington. With the exception of some fighting on May 22 at Gum Swamp below Kinston, Hill's withdrawal brought to an end the heavy fighting in eastern North Carolina for the year.

By the last of May most of the regiments operating in the State had been sent to Virginia. General Lee was preparing for his invasion of Pennsylvania, and there were urgent calls for the troops stationed in North Carolina. Early in May North Carolina troops had fought bravely at Chancellorsville, but at Gettysburg

The battle near Kinston on March 8, 1865. Frank Leslie's Illustrations in *The American Soldier in the Civil War.*

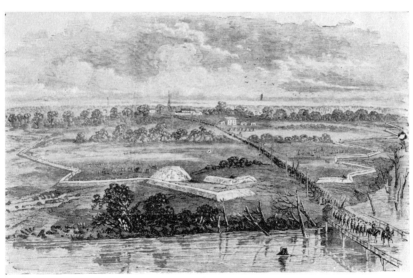

General John M. Schofield's army on its march toward Goldsboro, March, 1865. Frank Leslie's Illustrations in *The American Soldier in the Civil War.*

Brigadier General Junius Daniel (1828-1864), native of Halifax County; graduated from West Point in 1851; commissioned colonel of Fourteenth North Carolina Regiment, June, 1861; fought in Seven Days' campaign; appointed brigadier general, September, 1862, and stationed in Drewry's Bluff vicinity until sent to North Carolina in December, 1862; commanded his brigade at Gettysburg, the Wilderness, and Spotsylvania Court House where he was mortally wounded.

Major General Robert Frederick Hoke (1837-1912), native of Lincolnton; educated at Kentucky Military Institute; nephew of Colonel John F. Hoke; commissioned colonel of Twenty-first North Carolina Regiment in 1862; promoted major general in 1864; led division against Federal garrison and took town of Plymouth on April 20, 1864; troops bore the brunt of the fight at Bentonville and surrendered with General Joseph E. Johnston on April 26, 1865; appointed state director of the North Carolina Railroad; operated the Cranberry Iron Works; president of the North Carolina Home Insurance Company in Raleigh.

on July 1, 2, and 3 they were to reach "the pinnacle of military greatness. . . . Of the 15,301 Confederates killed and wounded . . . [in this battle] 4,033 wore North Carolina uniforms."

Chapter VII

FEDERAL OCCUPATION IN THE EAST—DISAFFECTION IN THE WEST, 1863

Even though military activity was at a minimum in North Carolina during the summer and fall of 1863, the times were gloomy. Lee's defeat at Gettysburg and the capture of Vicksburg cast a spell of despondency over the State. Also Editor W. W. Holden of the Raleigh *Standard* was carrying on an active campaign to bring the war to a close at any price. Peace meetings were held throughout the State, and soldiers were deserting in large numbers. In western North Carolina a veritable civil war existed between the Confederate troops on the one hand and organized deserters and "bushwackers" on the other. At the same time, the Federals in the eastern part of the State were stripping the "region of everything of value that was movable."

The eastern counties, lying open to the Federals, were subject to numerous enemy raids. In their forages into the country the Federal soldiers committed depredations of all sorts. Edward Stanly, Union governor of the State, in commenting on the conduct of the troops said: "Had the war in North Carolina been conducted by soldiers who were Christians and gentlemen, the state would long ago have rebelled against rebellion. But instead of that, what was done? Thousands and thousands of dollars' worth of property were conveyed North. Libraries, pianos, carpets, mirrors, family portraits, everything in short, that could be removed, was stolen by men abusing . . . slaveholders and preaching liberty, justice, and civilization."

The horror of Federal occupation was intensified by the activities of the "Buffaloes." In gangs of usually a dozen or so men, these native Union bushwackers infested the swamps. At night they liked to visit their former neighbors and perpetrate every "type of violence and crime."

Conditions became so bad in eastern North Carolina that some planters left their homes to seek refuge in the central part of the State. The majority of the people, however, remained on their farms, notwithstanding the fact that large numbers of slaves had fled to the Federal lines.

The central and western counties of the State, though free of enemy troops, also experienced difficult times. By the close of

Confederate soldier at Gettysburg, July 1, 2, and 3, 1863.

Confederate soldier, 1861-1865.

Confederate deserters in the mountains. *Pictorial War Record*, October 27, 1883.

1863, disaffection in these areas had reached an alarming stage. As early as November, 1861, Governor Clark had become concerned over conditions in western North Carolina. On this date he wrote the authorities in Richmond that he was receiving "numerous communications from the North Carolina counties bordering on East Tennessee" requesting help against traitors. Although the western part of the State had not been strong for secession, it showed great loyalty at the outbreak of war by furnishing an undue portion of volunteers. Such patriotism, however, stripped many areas of all young men and made it almost impossible for the mountain folk to protect themselves against native unionists, east Tennessee raiders, and various outlaw bands that had collected in the area to rob and steal

The bitter party spirit that developed in 1862 helped to increase dissatisfaction and disloyalty in the central and western counties. W. W. Holden, the influential newspaper editor, vigorously attacked Governor Clark's policy "of the last man and the last dollar," if necessary, to win the war. Holden urged the election of "peace men" in the August election, and for governor he supported Zebulon B. Vance, against William Johnston. Vance was thought to be the more conservative of the two candidates.

The agitation of Holden and his followers paid dividends. By March, 1862, it was necessary to send troops into Chatham County to arrest deserters. On every side it was said that extreme disloyalty existed in Davidson, Forsyth, Randolph, and Guilford counties. In Yadkin and Wilkes counties the disaffected men threatened to interfere with the coming elections. Farther west in Madison County General Kirby Smith had troops to deal with the large numbers of deserters in that area.

When the election was held, Vance won an easy victory over Johnston. In those central and western counties infested with deserters, Vance's margin of victory was great. This strong vote in the disaffected areas did not mean that the new governor wanted "Unionist" support. Not once during the campaign did he state that he agreed with the "peace" sentiments of Holden. For the *Fayetteville Observer* Vance expressed views to the contrary. In a letter to the paper he said: "Believing the only hope of the South depended upon the prosecution of the war at all hazards and to the utmost extremity so long as the foot of the invader pressed Southern soil, I took the field at an early day, with the determination to remain there until an independence was achieved. My convictions in this regard remain unchanged."

While the gubernatorial campaign of 1862 was in progress, the Confederate government passed the first of three laws that were to be particularly obnoxious to the mountain people. It was the Conscription Act of April, 1862, calling into the service for three years all white males between eighteen and thirty-five years of age. The other two laws, which brougnt the war forcibly home to the region, were the tax in kind and impressment acts passed in 1863. The first of these was a tithe to the government under which farmers were compelled to give one-tenth of all their produce for distribution by the authorities at Richmond. The second law gave specific committees the right to take livestock, slaves, provisions, and wagons for use by the Confederate army and to set the price that should be paid for them. For mountain folk, accustomed to individual freedom, these acts were especially galling. Of the three pieces of legislation the Conscription Act was detested the most. Having responded very generously to the early calls for troops, the mountain region was pretty well depleted of young blood by the time conscription went into effect. This additional demand for troops, therefore, met with considerable opposition.

A writer in Stokes County, protesting the call for more men, pointed out that the county had already enrolled thirteen hundred men, of whom eleven hundred were in service. The deprivations which had come to the women and children, he said, were almost unbelievable. The corn, wheat, rye, and oat crops were short, and the few men who had corn were afraid to let it go, for they did not know at what moment they too would have to leave their family to care for themselves. "If all the conscripts from my county are taken off," the writer continued, "it will be impossible for those left behind to make support for another year."

By the summer of 1863 opposition to conscription got practically beyond the control of the military. An inspector of conscription, writing from Salisbury at this time, stated that in Cherokee County a large body of deserters and those who were resisting conscription "had assumed a sort of military occupation, taking a town, and that in Wilkes County they had organized, drilling regularly, and were intrenched in a camp to the number of 500." The report also indicated that three or four hundred deserters were organized in Randolph County and that there were large numbers in Catawba, Yadkin, and Iredell counties. "Those who were liable to conscription," the inspector said, "lagged behind in proportion to those deserting." As a result of this situation, the enrollment officers went about their work "with the only hope that they would reach their goal by means of a military force." Unfortunately, troops for this type duty were seldom available.

From 1863 to the end of the war the problem of desertion clearly endangered the military operations of the Confederacy. By the spring of 1863 desertion had become a critical problem in the Army of Northern Virginia. On April 18 General Lee informed the Secretary of War that there had been "frequent desertion from the North Carolina Regiments." The soldiers continued to leave in such numbers that in May General Lee again wrote the Secretary about this matter, stating that unless desertions could be stopped immediately, the number of North Carolina troops in his army would be greatly reduced. From northern Virginia deserters usually followed the mountain ridges southward into western North Carolina or other mountain areas. They generally traveled in bands as they left the army and were heavily armed, making it almost impossible for the home guard to cope with them. Governor Vance estimated that there were twelve hundred deserters in the mountains in 1863. This situation led J. A. Campbell, Assistant Secretary of War, to write that the "condition of things in the mountain districts of North Carolina, South Carolina, Georgia, and Alabama menaces the existance of the Confederacy as fatally as either of the armies of the United States."

Federal authorities failed to capitalize on the critical state of affairs in the mountains of North Carolina. No large scale military operations took place in the area. On the other hand, violence and cruelty which appeared early in the mountain struggle prob-ably reached their height in February, 1863. The previous month a group of men from the Shelton Laurel section of Madison County had raided Marshall, the county seat, and plundered the stores. On hearing of the raid, Governor Vance immediately appealed for military aid. In response to this request General Henry Heth at Knoxville sent a force to Madison County to deal with the raiders. The officer commanding these troops had at least thirteen prisoners that he had taken along the Laurel River "shot to death under the most cold-blooded circumstances." This cruel act brought the entire area to fever pitch and Governor Vance demanded an official investigation.

The loss of east Tennessee in the fall of 1863 left western North Carolina open to the threat of constant raids and possibly a major invasion. To meet these threats General Robert B. Vance, brother of the Governor, was placed in command of the newly formed Western Military District of North Carolina. His orders were to "organize all troops raised in that district, both Confederate and State, and protect against raids on the railroad from Knoxville to Ashville." In October General Vance turned back a Federal force near the Tennessee line. After this success Vance took the offensive and conducted several forays into east Tennessee, but on one of these he was taken prisoner. A short time later Colonel J. B. Palmer replaced Vance as commander in western North Carolina and undertook the defense of the mountains.

The close of the year 1863 found North Carolina in a "deplorable" condition. With the coastal plains under Federal occupation and the mountains overrun with deserters, the State was at the mercy of the enemy.

Chapter VIII

PICKETT BEFORE NEW BERN, JANUARY-FEBRUARY, 1864

On January 2, 1864, General Lee wrote President Davis: "The time is at hand when if an attempt can be made to capture the enemy's forces at New Bern, it should be done. . . . A large amount of provisions and other supplies are said to be at New Bern, which are much wanted by the army, besides much that is reported in the country that will thus be made accessible to us." Davis, aware of the state of affairs in North Carolina, approved of Lee's plan and even went so far as to suggest that the General himself take command of the operation. Lee was hesitant to accept the position and suggested the North Carolinian, Robert F. Hoke as the best man for the job. Despite Lee's recommendation Hoke was not given the command. He was only a brigadier general, and it was thought that an officer of higher rank was needed to conduct a campaign of such large proportions. Thereupon Major General George E. Pickett was selected for the task. For command of the co-operating naval force President Davis selected his own aide, Commander John Taylor Wood.

A force of approximately thirteen thousand men, and seven navy cutters were soon concentrated at Kinston. General Pickett divided his troops into three commands and on the morning of January 30 moved in the direction of New Bern. General S. M. Barton, commanding one of the divisions, was directed to cross the Trent River near Trenton and proceed on the south side of this body of water to Brice's Creek below New Bern. After crossing the creek, he was to take the forts along the Neuse River and enter New Bern by way of the railroad bridge. Colonel James A. Dearing's cavalry was given the task of capturing Fort Anderson north of New Bern. General Pickett, with Robert F. Hoke's brigade and the remainder of the force, planned to advance on the coastal city from the west along the Dover road. A simultaneous attack by these three columns on the defenses of New Bern was planned for Monday morning. Commander Wood's orders were to engage the gunboats at New Bern and then to co-operate with the land forces in their attack on the city.

In carrying out this plan, General Hoke on Monday, February 1, drove in the Federal outpost at Batchelder's Creek. After crossing the stream, about ten miles west of New Bern, he moved his command to within a mile of the city and there halted to await the sound of Barton's guns from the opposite side of Trent River. Hoke waited in vain all day for some sign of activity below New Bern. Finally on Tuesday General Barton sent word that "the works [at Brice's Creek] . . . were too strong to attack and that he had made no advance and did not intend to. . . ." Colonel Dearing, whose orders were to capture Fort Anderson, also reported that he had found the Federal fortifications on his front too powerful to storm. Faced with the failure of two of his columns, Pickett withdrew his forces from New Bern.[1]

The naval operations conducted by Commander Wood were more successful. This daring officer with a picked crew dropped down the Neuse River from Kinston and on the night of February 1 boarded the Federal steamer "Underwriter" anchored at New Bern. After a bitter hand-to-hand fight with the ship's crew, the vessel was captured. Preparations were being made to move the "Underwriter" when it was learned that there was not enough steam in the boilers to get underway. This development, along with the harassing fire from a nearby fort, caused Commander Wood to burn his prize and retire. Even though the "Underwriter" had to be destroyed, its capture was the chief accomplishment of an otherwise ill-fated expedition.

---

[1] Two days before Pickett put his army in motion for New Bern, General J. G. Martin set out from Wilmington to attack the Federal garrison at Newport barracks near Shepherdsville. On February 2 he captured the barracks, seventy or eighty prisoners, and many stores. This was a complete victory, but it in no way compensated for Pickett's repulse.

Chapter IX

PLYMOUTH AND THE "ALBEMARLE," 1864

After the failure of the New Bern expedition, General Pickett returned to Virginia, and General Hoke took over command of the army. Immediately upon assuming his new duties, Hoke made plans for an attack upon Plymouth. This strategic little town near the mouth of the Roanoke River was protected on land by three thousand Federals under General H. W. Wessells and on water by four gunboats under Commander C. W. Flusser. In order to capture this place it was necessary for Hoke to have both land and naval forces at his disposal. Opportunely for him the Confederate navy had under construction at this time, at Edwards Ferry on the Roanoke River, an ironclad ram named the "Albemarle." In response to appeals from General Hoke, Confederate authorities allowed the ram to participate in the attack on Plymouth. On April 18 the "Albemarle," although still under construction, slipped from her moorings at Edwards Ferry and started down the river. In command of this strange-looking craft was Commander James W. Cooke, formerly an officer in the United States Navy.

As soon as Hoke was assured of the aid of the "Albemarle," he invested Plymouth on the land side and attacked the forts. Commander Flusser aboard the "USS Miami" at Plymouth reported on the 18th: "We have been fighting here all day. About sunset the enemy made a general advance along our whole line. They have been repulsed. . . . The ram will be down to-night or tomorrow. I fear for the protection of the town." The "Albemarle" arrived on the 19th and quickly proceeded to sink one gunboat and drive the others down the river, completely changing the tide of battle. The Federals could hold out only three days longer. On the 21st General Wessells surrendered his entire garrison, twenty-eight pieces of artillery, and large quantities of provisions. Jefferson Davis was so elated over this victory that he gave Hoke a battlefield promotion to major general.

The capture of Plymouth forced the Federal evacuation of nearby Washington but not before the town was burned by the retiring forces. So outrageous was the conduct of the Federal troops that one of their officers wrote: "It is well known that the army vandals did not even respect the charitable institutions but burst open the doors of the Masonic and Odd Fellows Lodge, pillaging them both and hawked about the streets the regalia and jewels. And this, too, by United States troops! It is well known that both public and private stores were entered and plundered and that devastation and destruction ruled the hour."

Following the victory at Plymouth, Hoke again turned his attention to New Bern. He had the city under attack when orders arrived in early May to abandon the siege and return to Virginia where Lee and Grant were locked in bitter struggle.

In the meantime the "Albemarle" threatened "the Federal control of the sounds and even menaced the blockade." To combat this danger Captain Melancthon Smith was hurriedly sent south with four large double-ended steamers. These vessels, along with those already in the Carolina waters, comprised quite a formidable squadron. Smith's orders were to hold the mouth of the Roanoke River at all costs. On May 5, about ten miles from the mouth of the river, the Federal squadron got its chance to engage the ram in combat. The Confederate craft, outnumbered, rammed, and subjected to terrific bombardment, put up a tremendous fight. Only when the "Albemarle" was unable to get up steam, because of a riddled smokestack, did she limp back to Plymouth. Even though disabled, the ram was still considered a menace by the Federals. Orders were soon out to destroy her at almost any price.

Federal authorities made several attempts to sink the "Albemarle," but all were unsuccessful. Finally the job was given to William B. Cushing, a bold, young naval officer.

On the night of October 27 Cushing, with a sizable party in two launches, steamed unnoticed up the river to Plymouth. The "Albemarle" at her mooring was protected by a thirty-foot boom of logs, and a fire on the shore illuminated the river. When the Federal party came within the light of the fire, Cushing ran his launch at full speed toward the boom. The launch slid over the logs, enabling the young officer to place a torpedo attached to a spar under the ram and explode it. The "Albemarle" sank, and the Federal launch, entangled in the boom, was captured along with its crew. Cushing, however, refusing to surrender, dived into the river and made his escape.

As a result of the destruction of the "Albemarle," Plymouth was recaptured by the Federals on October 31. Washington fell shortly thereafter. Thus, the sound region of the State was again under enemy domination.

The gunboat "Southfield" sinking after being run down by the ram "Albemarle." After disabling the "Southfield," the "Albemarle gave chase to the "Miami," but the latter retired below Plymouth after picking up several officers and men of the "Southfield." *Harper's Weekly*, May 7, 1864.

The capture of Plymouth, October 31, 1864. From a drawing.

The ironclad "Albemarle" was built on the banks of the Roanoke River and participated in the recapture of Plymouth, April 17-20, 1864, when Confederate forces under General Robert F. Hoke attacked the Federal forces which had been holding Plymouth since it was captured by them December 13, 1862. On October 27, 1864, the Federals again captured Plymouth, after the "Albemarle" had been torpedoed and sunk.

Captain James Wallace Cooke (1812-1869), native of Beaufort; entered United States Navy as midshipman in 1828; in 1861 sent to Roanoke Island and fought in battle of February 7, and near Elizabeth City; promoted commander and in 1863 ordered to Edwards Ferry on Roanoke River to superintend construction of ironclad "Albemarle," which he commanded in the recapture of Plymouth, April 20, 1864; promoted captain in 1864, and put in command of all naval forces in eastern North Carolina.

Smokestack of the ram "Albemarle" which engaged in several battles in North Carolina waters. This indicates how badly damaged the "Albemarle" was when it was finally sunk, October 27, 1864. Smokestack is on display in the Hall of History.

Chapter X

WESTERN NORTH CAROLINA, 1864

In western North Carolina during 1864, Confederate officials were fearful of cavalry raids from east Tennessee on the vital railroad lines just east of the mountains. To oppose such raids Colonel J. B. Palmer, in command of the region, had only the home guard, a few State troops, and less than five hundred Confederate soldiers.[1] Previously only one small Federal raiding party had reached as far as Murphy. In February, 1864, however, a detachment penetrated close to Franklin in Macon County, and in June of that year Colonel George W. Kirk led a daring raid from east Tennessee on Camp Vance near Morganton.

This camp for Confederate conscripts was completely surprised on the morning of June 28. Since rifles had not been issued to the recruits, the camp was easy prey for Kirk and his men. The Colonel's plan not only called for the capture of the Morganton garrison but also for the destruction of the important railroad bridge over the Yadkin River just north of Salisbury. This latter move was foiled when Confederate authorities at Salisbury were warned by telegraph of Kirk's presence in Burke County. With destruction of the Yadkin River bridge now out of the question, the Federals turned their attention to the large quantities of supplies and railroad equipment at Morganton. After destroying much railroad property and looting the town, Kirk returned to east Tennessee with considerable plunder and a number of prisoners. On his return Kirk successfully evaded a sizable Confederate force sent in pursuit.

By late 1864 the passes through the mountains were heavily guarded. Although this lessened considerably the chances of any more Federal raids, it did not reduce the problems on the home front. By this time disaffection and disloyalty in the area had multiplied by leaps and bounds. The mountains were so full of deserters that very little social stigma was attached to desertion, and the warm welcome accorded many a deserter caused the area to fill up with the disloyal from all the southern States. Formed into bands and heavily armed, these deserters plundered, murdered, and carried out every sort of outrage.

---

[1] Raids through the French Broad and Tennessee river passes were of primary concern to Colonel Palmer.

Violence reached a new stage in April, 1864, when the "Tory" [2] Montreval Ray and about seventy-five of his followers raided Burnsville while most of the men of the town were on military duty at Mars Hill in Madison County. Loyal Confederates were now intimidated to such an extent that some felt the "county is gone up."

For quite some time Governor Vance had been concerned over the state of affairs in western North Carolina. The Governor's erstwhile political ally, W. W. Holden, was responsible for much of the disaffection in the mountain areas, as well as the State as a whole. In 1863 Vance and Holden had parted ways over Holden's "peace" activities, and in the gubernatorial elections of 1864 these two men opposed each other in the race for governor. Holden, the "peace party" candidate, was soundly defeated by his opponent, who ran on a platform of "fight the Yankees and fuss with the Confederacy." [3] The Governor's efforts to curb desertions were none the less, generally unsuccessful. Even a promise of amnesty for all soldiers who would return to their units brought few returnees. Desertions continued to mount, and in some mountain localities loyal Confederates were forced to leave their homes and seek safety elsewhere. Conditions were so bad by December, 1864, that a resident of Henderson County reported that a state of anarchy existed in his county except where military forces were stationed.

As 1864 drew to a close, a feeling of depression was widespread among the people of North Carolina. Practically all of the males of conscript age were either in the service or in hiding. Bands of deserters roamed almost at will in the central and western counties. Much of the coastal region, with the exception of the Wilmington area, was under Federal control. In Georgia General William T. Sherman was preparing for a move through the Carolinas, after a successful "march to the sea," and in Virginia General Grant, after bloody engagements at the Wilderness, Spotsylvania, and Cold Harbor, had Lee pushed back to Petersburg.

---

[2] In western North Carolina, Union sympathizers were called "Tories."
[3] Vance, a strong believer in States' rights, was a bitter critic of President Davis throughout the war, but he was not a "peace" man, as was Holden.

Chapter XI

BLOCKADE-RUNNING, FORT FISHER, WILMINGTON, 1864-1865

The siege of Petersburg re-emphasized for the Federals the importance of eastern North Carolina to Lee's army. During the early stages of the war the Army of Northern Virginia drew immense quantities of supplies from this region. When Burnside overran much of eastern North Carolina in 1862, however, this source of supply was cut off. To make up for this shortage, provisions were brought into Wilmington through the blockade and shipped to Lee's army over the Wilmington and Weldon Railroad.

Wilmington, located twenty-eight miles up the Cape Fear River, was ideally located for blockade-running. It was free from enemy bombardment as long as the forts at the mouth of the river remained in Confederate hands. Moreover, there were two entrances to the Cape Fear. These channels were separated by Smith's Island, which was about ten miles long and located directly in the mouth of the river. North of the island was New Inlet, and south of it was Old Inlet. The distance between the passages was only six miles, but lying between them and jutting out into the Atlantic Ocean for about twenty-five miles was Frying Pan Shoals; therefore, a fleet guarding the two entrances had to cover a fifty-mile arc and at the same time stay out of range of Confederate shore batteries. Protecting New Inlet, the passage preferred by most vessels, were the extensive works known as Fort Fisher.[1] Guarding the lower passage were Forts Caswell and Campbell. On Smith's Island was Fort Holmes and up the river's west bank at Smithville and Old Brunswick, respectively, were Forts Johnston and Anderson.

The first blockading vessel to arrive near the mouth of the Cape Fear was the "Daylight," which took up position on July 20, 1861. By the fall of 1864 the number had increased to almost fifty. Confederate vessels, nevertheless, continued to slip through the blockade right up to the time of Fort Fisher's capture.

---

[1] Colonel William Lamb and General W. H. C. Whiting were primarily responsible for making Fort Fisher "the Gibraltar of America." Colonel Lamb took over command of the fort on July 4, 1862, and a year later General Whiting assumed command of the Wilmington district. Together these two officers pushed the preparation of the Cape Fear defenses, especially that of Fort Fisher.

The years 1863 and 1864 saw the greatest maritime activity in Wilmington. There are various estimates as to the number of ships that entered the port during this period. One source stated that 260 vessels visited Wilmington between May, 1863, and December, 1864. It is doubtful if correct information is available on the subject, but there can be little doubt that the traffic was heavy.

A few of the more successful blockade-runners were the "R. E. Lee," the "Siren," the "Kate," the "Bamsbee," and the "Advance." The latter was the only blockade-runner owned by the State of North Carolina. These ships and many others brought into the Confederacy voluminous supplies so necessary for the war effort. During the last months of the struggle, blockade-runners practically kept the Army of Northern Virginia in supplies. One writer states: "Near the end of the war half the food for Lee's Army came through the blockade to Wilmington. . . ." Federal authorities realized that they could strike Lee no more effective blow than by the capture of Wilmington, "and Lee, himself, warned the defenders of Forts Fisher and Caswell that if those forts fell he would be compelled to abandon his defenses of Richmond." The first attempt by the Union forces to reduce the defenses of Wilmington came in December, 1864.

When it became established that an attack was forthcoming, President Davis sent General Braxton Bragg, who had achieved few military successes, to Wilmington to take over command of the defenses of that area. General W. H. C. Whiting, formerly in command of the Wilmington district, was a capable officer and very well liked both by his men and the citizens of Wilmington.[2] The wisdom of the President's move, therefore, is highly questionable.

The long expected attack came at Christmas time, 1864. Since Fort Fisher was the key to the defenses of the Cape Fear area, it received the first Federal assault. General Benjamin F. Butler and Admiral David Porter, commanding the assaulting Union land and naval forces, respectively, were well aware of the fact that the capture of Fort Fisher would open the river to Federal gunboats and thereby make the other Confederate installations untenable.

The Union fleet appeared off the coast on December 20, but foul weather prevented any action until the evening of the 23rd.

---

[2] General Whiting was not removed from command, but General Bragg was placed over him.

Major General William Henry Chase Whiting (1824-1865), native of Mississippi; graduated from West Point in 1845; in November, 1862, took command of the military district of Wilmington; made the Cape Fear River a haven for blockade-runners, and developed Fort Fisher; promoted major general in February, 1863, and transferred to Petersburg; aided Colonel William Lamb in the defense of Fort Fisher where he was wounded in January, 1865, from which wounds he died March 10, 1865.

Colonel William Lamb (1835-1909), native of Norfolk, Virginia; graduated from William and Mary College in 1855; editor of the *Southern Argus* and engaged in newspaper work until 1861: in October, 1861, ordered to Wilmington, North Carolina; on July 4, 1862, placed in command of Fort Fisher where he kept up a gallant defense until its capture in 1865; returned to Norfolk after the war and achieved reputation as a vigorous writer.

The Confederate batteries at New Inlet near Wilmington as seen from the United States sloop "Iroquois." Sketch by James S. Rogers, U. S. Navy. *Harper's Weekly*, November 7, 1863.

The bombardment of Fort Fisher, January 13-15, 1865. Sketch by Frank Beard. *Pictorial War Record*, December 22, 1883.

The assault and capture of Fort Fisher, January 15, 1865. *Harper's Weekly*, February 4, 1865.

The Battle of Averasboro, March 16, 1865. *Harper's Weekly*, April 15, 1865.

During the night a boat loaded with 215 tons of powder was exploded within 200 yards of the fort. It was General Butler's belief that a mammouth explosion at the base of Fort Fisher would partially destroy the fortification, paralyze the defenders, and make capture the simple matter of occupancy.

The "powder boat" exploded around 1:45 A.M. on the 24th. The shock, much to Butler's dismay, was a far cry from what he had expected. Colonel William Lamb in immediate command at Fort Fisher, felt a slight shock and assumed that probably a blockade-runner had run aground and exploded.

Despite the failure of Butler's scheme, the Federal fleet moved into position on the morning of December 24 and began to bombard the fort. Also, during the day troops were landed up the peninsula from Fort Fisher. On Christmas day the land forces advanced to within seventy-five yards of the Confederate troops yet did not attack, General Butler having decided the defenses were impregnable. The General then ordered his forces to re-embark. Shortly thereafter, the Union fleet sailed away.

The Confederates were given little time to celebrate their victory for on January 12, 1865, the Federal fleet returned. Admiral Porter still commanded the naval squadron, but General Alfred H. Terry had replaced the incompetent Butler as leader of the land forces. On the morning of the 13th the Federal fleet began a determined bombardment of Fort Fisher. Suddenly at 3 P.M. on the 15th the firing ceased, and the steam whistles on all the vessels sounded. This was the signal for a column of United States sailors and marines which had landed above the fort to move to the attack. The defenders of Fort Fisher, under the courageous Colonel Lamb, repulsed this assault. Even so, before many shouts of victory could be raised, Federal battle flags were seen on the parapets to the west. While the sailors and marines had occupied the attention of Lamb and his men, a detachment of Federal soldiers almost unnoticed, gained a foothold in a weakly defended portion of the fort. This time the Federals were not to be turned back. Following some of the bitterest hand-to-hand fighting of the war, Fort Fisher capitulated at 9 P.M. on the 15th. Among the day's casualties were Colonel Lamb and General Whiting, who had entered the fort the previous day as a volunteer.

While the garrison at Fort Fisher was engaged in this life and death struggle, a sizable Confederate force under General Robert F. Hoke was at Sugar Loaf a few miles above the fort.

General Bragg, for various questionable reasons, would not order Hoke to Lamb's assistance. Because of this action, or lack of action, Bragg was severely criticized later.

With Fort Fisher in Federal hands, the Confederates were forced to abandon the other defense at the mouth of the Cape Fear. On the night of January 16 Fort Caswell was blown up. The installation on Smith's Island, and Forts Campbell and Johnston were also destroyed. This left only Fort Anderson up the river as a defense for Wilmington. The fort managed to hold out until February 20, at which time it was abandoned to the Federals under General Jacob D. Cox. The Confederates next made a stand on the north bank of Town Creek. In a brief skirmish General Johnson Hagood's Confederate force was defeated and driven back toward Wilmington.

The Federal troops continued their advance up the west bank of the Cape Fear River and by February 21 were across the river from Wilmington. The Confederate position at Sugar Loaf was now threatened from the north. Confronted with the possibility of having his escape route blocked, General Bragg ordered a retreat across Northeast River. This left the way open for the Federal troops on the east bank of the Cape Fear to enter Wilmington without opposition on the morning of February 22. Mayor John Dawson met the invaders and surrendered the city. The main body of the Federal army did not remain long in Wilmington but marched on in pursuit of General Bragg, who was moving toward Goldsboro.

Chapter XII

SHERMAN, STONEMAN, AND THE WAR'S END, 1865

In February, 1865, General John M. Schofield, newly appointed commander of Federal troops in eastern North Carolina, was under orders to make Goldsboro his ultimate objective and to open, as soon as possible, railroad communication between that city and the coast. Schofield was also to accumulate supplies for Sherman's army and to make junction with that fighting force at or near Goldsboro. Sherman at the time was marching northward through South Carolina.

At Wilmington General Schofield found very little rolling stock and few wagons. These shortages compelled him to operate from New Bern alone for the capture of Goldsboro. He first reinforced the garrison at New Bern and on February 28 ordered General Jacob D. Cox to take command there "and push forward at once." By March 6 Cox had a sizable force in motion for Goldsboro. Two days later at Southwest Creek below Kinston, he encountered the Confederates in force under General Bragg. On the 8th Bragg's men drove the Federals back three miles. Efforts to turn the Federal flanks on the 9th and 10th, however, were unsuccessful. A Confederate withdrawal followed.

At Goldsboro Bragg's troops were turned over to General Joseph E. Johnston who had been assigned in February to command the Army of Tennessee[1] and all the troops in the Department of South Carolina, Georgia, and Florida. It was Johnston's plan to concentrate his forces, which were scattered from Mississippi to the Carolinas, at some place in North Carolina and there strike one of Sherman's columns on the move. The Federal order of march by wings or corps, frequently a day's march from each other, justified Johnston's hope of striking one of the units when the others were not in supporting distance. This strategy was absolutely necessary because of the great discrepancy in the size of the opposing forces. Johnston could hope for a little more than twenty thousand men, whereas Sherman's veterans numbered three times that many.

While Sherman's army swept through South Carolina practically unopposed, a wave of despondency hit North Carolina.

---

[1] Only the shell of this once fine army remained. At Nashville, Tennessee, in December, 1864, the Army of Tennessee had been cut to pieces by a Union force under General George Thomas.

This despair was largely the result of Sherman's revolutionary method of waging war. This new concept, now known as "total war," called for attacks not only upon the armies in the field but also upon the civilians at home. It was war in its cruelest, though most efficient form.

By March 8 Sherman had his entire army on North Carolina soil in the vicinity of Laurel Hill Church.[2] Two days later at Monroe's Cross-Roads[3] below Fayetteville, Johnston's cavalry chiefs, Wade Hampton and Joe Wheeler, fought a spirited engagement with the Federal horsemen under Judson Kilpatrick. By engaging Kilpatrick in battle, Hampton and Wheeler were able to open the road to Fayetteville, which the Federal camp blocked. On the night of the 10th the Confederate cavalry joined General William J. Hardee near Fayetteville. Hardee's small force, after evacuating Charleston on February 18, had been moving north just ahead of Sherman's advancing army.

Fayetteville received severe treatment at Federal hands. Sherman's notorious "bummers"[4] pillaged much of the town before it could be garrisoned. When order was restored, numerous public buildings, including the arsenal, were burned.

At Fayetteville Sherman crossed the Cape Fear River. He then turned his army east toward Goldsboro, his destination since leaving Georgia. From Savannah to Fayetteville Sherman made very few mistakes, but from the latter place to Goldsboro he became careless. He placed little importance on Hardee's delaying action at Averasboro on March 16.[5] Also, he allowed his columns to become strung out to such extent that Johnston came close to crushing one of the Federal corps at Bentonville. At this small town west of Goldsboro Johnston had skillfully managed, on the 19th, to concentrate his scattered forces. Completely ignorant of this Confederate move, Sherman allowed

---

[2] Laurel Hill Church is located in Scotland County. In 1865 Scotland was part of Richmond County.

[3] Monroe's Cross-Roads is today on the Fort Bragg reservation.

[4] When Sherman commenced his march through the Carolinas in January, 1865, he cut himself off completely from his base at Savannah and made preparations to live off the land. His army of sixty thousand, therefore, had to forage liberally on the countryside as it pushed northward. To regulate the foraging parties, very strict orders were issued, yet there was a wide discrepancy between these orders and the actions of some of the men. Many of the foraging parties degenerated into marauding bands of robbers which operated not under the supervision of an officer but on their own. These self-constituted foragers, known as "bummers," committed most of the pillage and wanton destruction of property in North Carolina.

[5] This delaying action turned into an all day fight known as the Battle of Averasboro.

Major General John McAllister Schofield (1831-1906), native of New York; graduated from West Point in 1853; commanded departments of Missouri, Ohio, and North Carolina; by close of May, 1865, had organized county police, provided for local administration of justice, published regulations concerning freedmen, and established martial justice to restrain grave violations of law; served as Secretary of War during impeachment of Andrew Johnson; named major general in 1869; superintendent of West Point, 1876-1881; served as commander in chief of the army, 1888-1895.

Admiral David Dixon Porter (1813-1891), native of Pennsylvania; formal education was limited; in Mexican War served at Veracruz and Tabasco; in Civil War commanded mortar fleet at New Orleans and on Mississippi in 1862; aided in reduction of Vicksburg in 1863; commanded naval forces in attack on Fort Fisher in December, 1864, and January, 1865; superintendent of United States Naval Academy, 1865-1869; promoted admiral on August 15, 1870; chairman of naval board of inspection from 1877-1891.

General Joseph Eggleston Johnston (1807-1891), native of Virginia; graduated from West Point in 1829; served in the Black Hawk expedition and the Seminole and Mexican wars; joined the Confederate army, April, 1861; commanded Department of the Potomac; appointed general in August, 1861; in 1862 commanded Department of the West; took command of the Army of Tennessee in 1865 and led it through the Carolinas campaign; on April 18, 1865, signed armistice with General W. T. Sherman and surrendered April 26, 1865.

General William Tecumseh Sherman (1820-1891), native of Ohio; graduated from West Point in 1840; stationed in California during Mexican War; superintendent of military school in Louisiana; participated in Bull Run campaign, Shiloh, Vicksburg, Chattanooga, Atlanta, March to the Sea, and Carolinas campaigns; in March, 1869, succeeded Ulysses S. Grant as commander in chief of the army and held this position for fourteen years.

his 14th Corps to be surprised by Johnston. For awhile it looked as though the Confederates would carry the day, but Federal reinforcements late in the afternoon blunted the Confederate offensive. More Union troops reached the field during the 20th, and by the 21st Sherman had his entire army at Bentonville. That night Johnston withdrew his forces to Smithfield.

Sherman was victorious at Bentonville, the largest battle of the war fought on North Carolina soil, yet he failed to follow up his success by pursuing the enemy. Instead he marched his army into Goldsboro. Awaiting him there were the forces of Generals Terry and Cox of Schofield's command, which had marched up from Wilmington and New Bern, respectively.

At Goldsboro Sherman was disturbed to find neither the railroad from the coast repaired nor the supplies awaiting him. By March 24 repairs on the track from New Bern were finished, and the first train arrived in Goldsboro from the coast.

This completed the task Sherman set out to do upon leaving Savannah. His army was now united with those of Schofield. Large supply bases on the North Carolina coast were available by rail, and the countryside from Savannah to Goldsboro, for an average breadth of forty miles, had been laid waste.

Sherman now decided it was time to discuss with Grant the plans for a junction of their armies around Richmond. He hoped to share with the Army of the Potomac the glory of capturing the Confederate capital. Late in the afternoon of March 25 Sherman boarded a train for City Point, Virginia, Grant's headquarters.

A short time before Sherman departed for Virginia, General George Stoneman, with a six-thousand-man cavalry force, left east Tennessee for a raid through southwest Virginia and western North Carolina.[6] His primary objectives were the Virginia and Tennessee Railroad in Virginia and the Danville-Greensboro line in North Carolina.

Stoneman's advance guard arrived at Boone, North Carolina, on March 28. The local citizens thinking Federal cavalrymen no closer than fifty miles were completely surprised by the raid. General A. C. Gillem, Stoneman's second in command, destroyed some public property but inflicted very little damage on private dwellings.

---

[6] Stoneman had originally been ordered to assist Sherman in the Carolinas by a raid on Columbia, South Carolina. By the time he was ready to move, Sherman was well into North Carolina; therefore the Columbia raid was abandoned.

General Stoneman with the bulk of his force moved out of Boone on March 28 and proceeded through Deep Gap to Wilkesboro. Gillem, leading a smaller party, left Boone, went to Blowing Rock, and down the mountain toward Lenoir. The split force was united at Wilkesboro by the evening of March 29. Here it remained for two days.

On March 31 Stoneman moved north toward Virginia, passing through Mount Airy on April 2 and 3. After destroying much railroad mileage in the area of Christiansburg, Virginia, Stoneman reunited his scattered forces and fell back to Danbury in Stokes County, North Carolina.

On the evening of April 9 the day Lee surrendered at Appomattox, Stoneman's cavalry was passing through Germantown. The next day the First Brigade under Colonel W. J. Palmer occupied Salem. From here Stoneman sent out detachments in all directions to destroy railroad property, cotton, and government stores.

After leaving Salem, Stoneman moved through Mocksville to Salisbury. At Grant's Creek a few miles north of Salisbury, approximately five hundred men under General W. M. Gardner offered what resistance they could to the Federal force but were easily pushed aside.

Salisbury was a rich prize for Stoneman. Even though he failed in his attempt to level the important railroad bridge across the nearby Yadkin River, the Federal Commander did destroy in the town vast quantities of military stores, railroad property, public buildings, and the Confederate prison. For several weeks past, the thought of freeing their comrades imprisoned at Salisbury had spurred Stoneman's troopers on toward this Rowan County town. In November, 1861, a vacated cotton factory in Salisbury had been turned into a prison. By the latter months of the war ten thousand men crowded its quarters. This overtaxing of facilities and a shortage of supplies had resulted in a staggering mortality rate. Because of these conditions Confederate authorities decided to remove the prisoners as soon as a safe place could be found for them. The news of Stoneman's activities, plus the government's need for workshops, hastened the action. By March, 1865, all of the prisoners had been transferred, thereby leaving for Stoneman's anxious soldiers only the opportunity to raze a few abandoned prison buildings.

On the 13th, his work at Salisbury finished, Stoneman turned west toward Tennessee. Two days later he was in Lenoir, having

The Battle of Bentonville, March 19-21, 1865. *Harper's Weekly*, April 15, 1865.

passed through Statesville and Taylorsville on the way. At Lenoir Stoneman remained forty-eight hours and then departed for Tennessee. He took with him only enough troops to guard his prisoners. Colonel Palmer had already been sent off with a sizable force to raid the Charlotte area, and General Gillem was under orders to move with the remainder of the command directly on Asheville. Gillem took Morganton on the 18th, after a skirmish on the upper Catawba, and on the following day arrived at Marion. A Confederate force under General J. G. Martin blocked his attempt to reach Asheville by way of Swannanoa Gap west of Marion. This compelled Gillem to turn south and cross the mountains at Howard's Gap. After passing through the gap, he raided Hendersonville, and by the 25th was in Asheville. Unknown to Gillem, Sherman and Johnston had signed an armistice on the 18th. The news of this momentous event was slow in reaching the western part of the State.

General Sherman, as previously pointed out, had visited Grant at his City Point headquarters during the latter part of March in the hope of organizing a joint offensive against Lee. His mission proved futile as the Commander-in-Chief was not willing to delay his own push against the Confederates at Richmond until Sherman's troops at Goldsboro could arrive. Back at his North Carolina base, Sherman began preparations for a move against Johnston, who was thought to be somewhere between Goldsboro and Raleigh. On April 10 the Federal army moved out of its base in the direction of Raleigh. When Johnston, who was bivouacked at neighboring Smithfield, learned of this move, he also put his small army in motion for the North Carolina capital.

During the night of the 11th Sherman learned of Lee's surrender at Appomattox. The announcement of this startling news the next day put the Federal soldiers in a hilarious mood, even as the march went forward. That night spirits were further heightened when peace commissioners from Raleigh arrived in camp and conferred with Sherman about the peaceful surrender of the capital city.

By this time Raleigh had been evacuated by the Confederate troops, and Johnston had reported to President Davis at Greensboro. The General was fully convinced that his small army, its ranks growing thinner by the day, was no match for Sherman. After considerable discussion, he was able to get the Chief Executive to authorize him to send Sherman a communication asking for a suspension of hostilities. This led to a meeting between Sherman and Johnston at the small Bennett home, a few miles west of Durham. There on April 17 and 18 the Union General granted his adversary the most generous terms.

Sherman assumed his terms would be acceptable to the administration in Washington. He soon learned otherwise. This necessitated a second meeting at the Bennett farmhouse where, on the 26th, Sherman granted and Johnston accepted terms similar to those Lee had received at Appomattox. If the agreement first offered to General Johnston had been accepted by the civil authorities in the North, the southern people would have resumed the place they held in the Union in 1861, and the evils of Radical Reconstruction might have been avoided. Still, Sherman had the satisfaction of knowing he had tried to befriend the South, when she laid down her arms.

Fighting continued for two more weeks in western North Carolina. On April 26 a portion of General Gillem's command thoroughly ransacked Asheville, and on May 9, at Waynesville, a small Confederate force under Colonel J. R. Love skirmished with a Union cavalry detachment. These were the last shots of the war fired on North Carolina soil.

From the battle of Hatteras to the skirmish at Waynesville, four long and trying years, North Carolina served as a battleground for the armies of a divided nation. Although the numbers involved in these engagements were comparatively small, the battles themselves were not unimportant in the big military picture. Lee's operations in Virginia were controlled to a large extent by the fact that North Carolina was his chief source of supply. The Federal occupation of much of the State's coastal region after 1861 was of more than minor concern to the Confederate Commander, since Union troops in this area were a constant threat to the vital communication lines running south from Richmond. General Lee's dependence upon North Carolina both for supplies and for protection to his rear gave the State an important role, yet ofttimes overlooked, in the grand strategy of the war.

No words are needed for the story this picture tells.

Negotiations between Generals W. T. Sherman and Joseph E. Johnston, April 18, 1865, at the Bennett House near the present city of Durham. Also present were General Judson Kilpatrick, Confederate General Wade Hampton and their staffs. Frank Leslie's Illustrations in *The American Soldier in the Civil War*.

SOME BOOKS ABOUT THE CIVIL WAR

Ammen, Daniel, *The Atlantic Coast*. New York, 1883.

Anderson, Mrs. John H., *North Carolina Women of the Confederacy*. Fayetteville, 1926.

Arthur, John P., *Western North Carolina A History from 1730 to 1913*. Raleigh, 1914.

Ashe, Samuel A. Court, *History of North Carolina*, Volume II. Raleigh, 1925.

Barrett, John G., *Sherman's March Through the Carolinas*. Chapel Hill, 1956.

Clark, Walter (ed.), *Histories of the Several Regiments and Battalions from North Carolina in the Great War, 1861-'65*, 5 volumes. Raleigh, 1901.

Connor, Robert D. W., *North Carolina, Rebuilding an Ancient Commonwealth*. Volume II. New York, 1929.

Dykeman, Wilma, *The French Broad*. New York, 1955.

Hamilton, J. G. de Roulhac, *Reconstruction in North Carolina* (Volume LVIII, Columbia University Faculty [ed.], *Studies in History, Economics and Public Law*). New York, 1914.

Hill, Daniel H., *A History of North Carolina in the War Between the States*, 2 volumes. Raleigh, 1926.

Hill, Daniel H., *North Carolina* (Volume IV, *Confederate Military History*). Atlanta, 1899.

Johnson, Robert U. and Clarence C. Buel (eds.), *Battles and Leaders of the Civil War*, 4 volumes. New York, 1888.

Massachusetts Memorial to Her Soldiers and Sailors Who Died in the Department of North Carolina, 1861-1865. Boston, 1909.

Operations on the Atlantic 1861-1865 (Volume IX, *Papers of the Military Historical Society of Massachusetts*). Boston, 1912.

Sitterson, Joseph C., *The Secession Movement in North Carolina* (Volume XXIII, Albert R. Newsome [ed.], *The James Sprunt Studies in History and Political Science*). Chapel Hill, 1939.

Sloan, John A., *North Carolina in the War Between the States*. Washington, 1883.

Spencer, Cornelia P., *The Last Ninety Days of the War in North Carolina*. New York, 1886.

Sprunt, James, *Chronicles of the Cape Fear River, Being Some Account of Historic Events on the Cape Fear River*. Raleigh, 1914.

Stick, David, *The Outer Banks of North Carolina*. Chapel Hill, 1958.

Tatum, Georgia L., *Disloyalty in the Confederacy*. Chapel Hill, 1934.

Waddell, Alfred M., *The Last Year of the War in North Carolina, Including Plymouth, Fort Fisher, and Bentonville*. Richmond, 1888.

Yates, Richard E., *The Confederacy and Zeb Vance* (Volume VIII, William S. Hoole [ed.], *Confederate Centennial Studies*). Tuscaloosa, 1958.